ROUTLEDGE LIBRARY EDITIONS: LIBRARY AND INFORMATION SCIENCE

Volume 66

PERSONNEL ISSUES IN REFERENCE SERVICES

PERSONNEL ISSUES IN REFERENCE SERVICES

Edited by
BILL KATZ AND RUTH A. FRALEY

LONDON AND NEW YORK

First published in 1986 by The Haworth Press, Inc.

This edition first published in 2020
by Routledge
2 Park Square, Milton Park, Abingdon, Oxon OX14 4RN

and by Routledge
52 Vanderbilt Avenue, New York, NY 10017

Routledge is an imprint of the Taylor & Francis Group, an informa business

© 1986 The Haworth Press, Inc.

All rights reserved. No part of this book may be reprinted or reproduced or utilised in any form or by any electronic, mechanical, or other means, now known or hereafter invented, including photocopying and recording, or in any information storage or retrieval system, without permission in writing from the publishers.

Trademark notice: Product or corporate names may be trademarks or registered trademarks, and are used only for identification and explanation without intent to infringe.

British Library Cataloguing in Publication Data
A catalogue record for this book is available from the British Library

ISBN: 978-0-367-34616-4 (Set)
ISBN: 978-0-429-34352-0 (Set) (ebk)
ISBN: 978-0-367-37410-5 (Volume 66) (hbk)
ISBN: 978-0-367-37411-2 (Volume 66) (pbk)
ISBN: 978-0-429-35365-9 (Volume 66) (ebk)

Publisher's Note
The publisher has gone to great lengths to ensure the quality of this reprint but points out that some imperfections in the original copies may be apparent.

Disclaimer
The publisher has made every effort to trace copyright holders and would welcome correspondence from those they have been unable to trace.

Personnel Issues
in Reference Services

Edited by
Bill Katz and Ruth A. Fraley

The Haworth Press
New York • London

Personnel Issues in Reference Services has also been published as *The Reference Librarian*, Number 14, Spring/Summer 1986.

Copyright © 1986 by The Haworth Press, Inc. All rights reserved. Copies of articles in this publication may be noncommercially reproduced for the purpose of educational advancement. Otherwise, no part of this work may be reproduced or utilized in any form or by any means, electronic or mechanical, including photocopying, microfilm, and recording, or by any information storage and retrieval system, without permission in writing from the publisher. Printed in the United States of America.

The Haworth Press, Inc., 28 East 22 Street, New York, NY 10010-6194
EUROSPAN/Haworth, 3 Henrietta Street, London WC2E 8LU England

Library of Congress Cataloging-in-Publication Data

Personnel issues in reference services.

    Includes bibliographical references.
    1. Reference librarians—Addresses, essays, lectures. 2. Library personnel management—Addresses, essays, lectures. 3. Reference services (Libraries)—Addresses, essays, lectures. I. Katz, William A.,
1924-   . II. Fraley, Ruth A.
Z682.4.R44P47 1986   025.5   86-3063
ISBN 0-86656-523-X

Personnel Issues in Reference Services

The Reference Librarian
Number 14

CONTENTS

Introduction   xiii
    Ruth Fraley

OVERVIEW

The Current Trends and Controversies in the Literature of Reference Services and Their Implications for the Practice of Reference Work   1
    Carl F. Orgren
    James Rice

Library-Use Instruction	2
Online Searching	3
Special Reference Services	5
Standards and Guidelines	6
The Impact of Technical Services on Reference Services	7
Resource Sharing	8
Professionalism	9

WHO WILL WORK THE PUBLIC SERVICE DESKS?

Selecting, Training and Retaining Staff for the Library's Public Service Desks   19
    Carol Lee Anderson

Selecting Staff for the Service Desk	20
Initial Training	22
On-going Training	25
Retaining Staff	26
Scheduling	28
Not a Replacement for the Reference Desk	29

Choosing How to Staff the Reference Desk   31
John Montag

   Local Choice   32
   Quality of Service   32
   Training, Education, and Staffing   34
   Personnel Policies, Salaries, and Equity   35
   Conclusion   36

End-User Searching: The Beginning or the End?   39
Geraldene Walker

   New Information Sources   40
   System Adaptations   40
   Software Packages   43
   End-User Searching   43
   Library Alternatives   46
   Other Opportunities   49

Staff Sharing: A Development Program   53
Joan W. Jensen

   The Reference Assistant Program   55
   Staff Sharing in Perspective   58

The Reference Librarian in the Small Information Center: Selection and Training   61
Miriam H. Tees

   Qualifications for the Job   62

ADMINISTRATION, EVALUATION, AND STAFF TRAINING

The Reference Librarian as Personnel Administrator   73
William Miller

   Learning to Get Along   75
   Not the Best of Conditions   76
   The Clerical Staff Role   78
   Performance Evaluation   79
   Role Models Needed   80
   Recipe for Success   82

Evaluating the Reference Librarian   85
Sara B. Sluss

A "Fair" Evaluation	86
Reluctance to Evaluate	86
Problems of Evaluating Services	88
LAMA Guidelines	89
Documenting Tasks and Functions	90
Goals Development	91
Informal Conference	93
Formal Evaluation Conference	93
Trusting the Process	94
Evaluating Quality	95
Satisfactory vs. Superior	95

Time Management for Information Services   97
Bill Bailey

The Corporate Clock	97
The IS Clock	99
An Immodest Proposal	100
On Desk Duty	100
Off Desk Duty	101
Conclusion	102

Role of the Manager in Reference Staff Development   105
Margaret Hendley

Introduction and Overview	105
Definition of Terms	106
Needs Assessment	107
Policies and Budgets	107
Communication to Staff	108
Funding for Staff Development	108
Job Environment	109
Motivation of Staff	109
Individuality of Staff	110
Two "Streams" of Development: Subject Specialization and Supervisory/Management	110
Opportunities for Staff Development Internal to the System	111
Involvement in Committees	111
Participatory Management	112

Library Workshops	113
Job Rotation	113
External Opportunities	113
Participation in Committees External to System	114
Job Exchange	115
Planning for Your "Graduates"	115
Performance Appraisal	116
Conclusion	116

Quality Control of Reference Service in Branch Libraries of a Multi-Campus College — 119
  Pamela L. Wonsek

Establishing the Goals	120
Centralization and Uniformity	120
Decentralization and Autonomy	121
MBO in Planning and Control	122
Accountability and Performance Appraisal	123
Critical Incident Process	124
Hiring New Staff	125
Training New Staff	125
Developing Independence and Autonomy	126
Communication and Feedback	127
Building an Effective Branch Team	128
Observing the Library Service	129

PREPARATION FOR THE JOB, RECRUITMENT, CONTINUING EDUCATION AND OTHER CONCERNS

Everybody Needs Information — 133
  Miles M. Jackson

Information Diffusion	134
Information Needs	135
Dervin's Findings	136

Multiple Roles of Academic Reference Librarians: Problems of Education and Training — 141
  Barbara E. Kemp

The Recruitment, Selection and Retention of Academic Reference Librarians   **151**
    Ilene F. Rockman

Characteristics of a Reference Librarian	151
Recruitment	152
Selection	154
Retention	156
Conclusion	157

Reference Librarians as Teachers: Ego, Ideal and Reality in a Reference Department   **159**
    Ellen Broidy

Administration of Instruction Programs	160
Recruiting, Interviewing, Hiring	164
Evaluation and Training	167
Should All Reference Librarians Teach?	169

Microcomputer Continuing Education Training Will Assist Reference Librarians   **173**
    Thomas E. Alford

Revolution in Libraries	174
Online Service	176

Empirical Indications for Choosing Reference Librarianship as a Profession: A Biographical Approach   **181**
    Martin H. Sable

Primary-School Experience	182
Junior-High School Experience	182
High-School Experience	183
University Experience	183
Graduate School Experience	184
Decision to Enter Librarianship	185
Positions and Publications	185
Conclusion: The Hypotheses Revisited	187

Definitions Help   **191**
    Lora Landers

Background Information	191
Tiered Service	193

The Reference Librarian	194
Conclusion	195

Selecting a Reference Librarian: Signs to Look For in Selection   197
    Mabel Shaw
    Susan S. Whittle

Responsibility is Basic	198
Desirable Traits	199

Introduction

Ruth Fraley

Since Reference is a labor intensive activity it logically follows that many of the complications and considerations involved in the operation of a reference department are personnel issues. The number of possible combinations and permutations of these problems is quite large. Therefore, any compilation of articles about personnel in reference services will include a broad range of topics and when the collection is complete, there will always be the feeling that something is missing. Personnel matters are also among those most easily critiqued, second guessed and opposed by those not directly responsible for the decision. Very often, the perceived "correct" way to handle a major library problem as determined by consensus on the gossip network, involves a change in personnel matters. Just as often problems in libraries from poor morale to excessive absenteeism, to low productivity and turnover evolve from a combination of factors, the major one being poor personnel skills on the part of management. These skills or lack thereof become glaring during periods of austerity when every operation must be carefully scrutinized. Reduced staffing levels, added responsibilities without added rewards, and the pressures of trying to do more of the same with fewer resources highlight both the weak manager and the weak staff member. A cycle of negatives can ensue and the result will be a decrease in support from those who constitute the library community. One of the most difficult parts of administration is to take unpleasant or unpopular action, and often this type of action will involve a personnel issue. If the action must be implemented when the library is being managed by people with poor personnel skills, the negative situation is amplified. In addition, there is no single formula for successful personnel administration; what works in one library will fail abysmally in another. What works with one person, for that matter, will fail when attempted with another. All of the problems and misunderstandings can easily be exacerbated when the manager adopts a style or technique or practice which he or she is not only ill suited to implement but also does not believe to be a good and effective procedure. When there are problems on the front line, the primary point where staff and the library users interact, it will not be long before they spread and the entire library is in the quagmire.

A good place to start to tackle the overall question of library personnel, therefore is to look at the personnel issues affecting those who work at the service desks: the front line. While no facile solutions to any one of the several problems leap from these pages, there is a recognition of the wide scope of issues to consider and some part of the discussion will relate to almost every situation, directly or indirectly.

Orgren and Rice begin by tackling the difficult question of a definition of reference service and the major issues discussed in the literature during the last 10 to 15 years. Library instruction, online use, special services, standards, automation, and so on are briefly discussed while they consider the most important question to be that of professionalism. What *does* constitute a professional librarian? This is a major question because the hiring, firing, and supervision of a person must depend on the expectations of the position and until a professional librarian is defined in a manner realistic enough for supervisors to be able to use, surely the personnel issues and concerns required for daily operations are more complex and obtuse.

A good place to begin is to look at the individuals who are already working at the service desks in the library. Many service desks in a library are not staffed by professional librarians, can the patrons tell the difference? Anderson presents good pointers for hiring and training non-professional personnel who must work on service desks and suggests mechanisms to help these people work within the framework of a library with professional librarians assigned to work at the reference desk. The discussion continues as Montag asks some interesting questions about paraprofessionals at the reference desk and presents arguments for both points of view. Walker looks to the not too distant future sounding a clear warning about the probable impact of the ubiquitous microcomputer on the knowledge and expectations of patrons. Jenson talks about a successful program of job sharing within a library, increasing the pool of people able to work the service desks and providing change and variety in job responsibilities for all library staff. The characteristics needed for a reference librarian in the small special library where it is not always assumed or probable the MLS will be listed as a basic requirement for the position are summarized and presented by Tees. She also includes a strong recommendation for communicating with potential small special libraries so an appreciation of the MLS can be encouraged.

In the section on Administration, Miller presents some candid thoughts about the problems inherent in managing and supervising a reference department, especially when the manager has no control over the traditional rewards and motivators: money, position, and time. Sluss talks about the knotty problems of evaluating a professional when there are no traditional, measurable products like the proverbial defective widget but only subjective opinions. Bailey has some concrete suggestions about time management and accurately points out the impossibility of accomplishing anything other than desk duty when there is an excessive number of scheduled desk hours per person. He also discusses the loss, in this case, of time to contribute to the profession and to keep up to date. A considerable loss to the profession is implicit in his statement when individuals who have much to contribute are unable to do so. Hendley looks at many of the same questions and adds more to the concept of staff development as a responsibility of the reference department manager. The department manager whose job includes supervising librarians in several branch libraries has another set of slightly different problems and considerations. Wonsek provides a specific plan for interacting in this situation including suggestions for techniques to use to insure adequate communication as well as evenly distributed responsibility without stifling creativity. She recognizes the need for different types of libraries while remaining under the umbrella of the central library system.

The question of adding more with less not only increases stress but it also forces departments and libraries to make choices about priorities. Since this situation is occurring at the same time as rapid technological developments are changing the nature of expectations, sometimes the alternatives are neither evenly balanced nor clear choices. Walker suggests the choices may be made for us and the nature of reference services is due to change dramatically. Kemp looks at the question now and recognizes there are options for managers and reference librarians, many of these options must be exercised at the point of employment. Recruitment and all of its difficulties and chancy situations is an increasingly important aspect of reference service as a library able to hire only one person when the demands of the operation could justify three *must* make the correct hiring decision the first time as the costs and time involved in a poor decision are excessive. Rockman and Landers look at specific library operations and each outlines procedures and requirements for the positions, while Broidy and Alford talk about specific characteristics required for reference librarians. Broidy talks about the processes and mechanics of hiring people for instruction and reference. Alford points out the absolute necessity for familiarity with microcomputers and their applications for not only the new staff but also the existing staff. Sable's personalized account of what leads a person to become a librarian contrasts with Shaw and Whittle's discussion of desirable characteristics and requirements for the job.

The diversity of scope and coverage of topics in this collection are merely a small dent in the greater issue of personnel management of reference services but they are a beginning.

OVERVIEW

The Current Trends and Controversies in the Literature of Reference Services and Their Implications for the Practice of Reference Work

Carl F. Orgren
James Rice

Reference work by virtue of its nature deals with all kinds of information in all disciplines and attempts to provide it to all sorts of people for all sorts of reasons. While the very definition of reference service is a matter of controversy, we will open with an arbitrary one—the actions, and the administration of those actions, by which we assist patrons in their discovery and use of appropriate portions of mankind's graphic record. Note that the definition doesn't say appropriate to what—appropriate to the education, entertainment, edification, growth, etc. of the patron. These are intentionally left out because they are all relevant to our role, and the role of the library. Further, it is very difficult to separate them—who is to say a person well entertained isn't learning something? Who is to say there is not entertainment value in something learned? With this much diversity in the character of reference work, how can its literature be anything but diverse? Therefore we looked at the topic carefully but selectively to provide some semblance of order. Breadth is emphasized more than exhaustive depth. This will not be an enumeration of research studies, publications, or names of all writers on the subject. Instead, it is an overview of the primary issues that have been prominent in the literature and in the field during the last 10-15 years.

Mr. Orgren is Director, School of Library Science, The University of Iowa, Iowa City, IA 52242. Mr. Rice is a member of the faculty of the same school.

© 1986 by The Haworth Press, Inc. All rights reserved.

LIBRARY-USE INSTRUCTION

Certainly one of the most significant issues in reference work is library-use instruction and bibliographic instruction. The development of teaching library-use has, as primary foundations, the library college concept and the more general conviction that the library and library-use are central to all education. The movement evolved somewhat slowly during the 1950's and 1960's, with intensified efforts in the 1970's. For the last 10 years it has played a prominent role in the literature—in one study, around 1/3 of all the literature relating to reference service in academic libraries.[1] The practice of library-use instruction is gaining momentum in all types of libraries in various ways.

At the heart of the argument in favor of library-use instruction are two ideas. First is the notion that, while it is nice to teach people specific parts of any discipline, it is even better to teach them how to find out on their own—knowing how to catch a fish is better than receiving the fish. Of course, this is why library-use instruction has been most accepted in educational environments. The other rationale for library-use instruction is the idea that information is a valuable commodity in all environments—not just education. Information is power—and libraries have a unique role in the information explosion. As librarians, we have a responsibility to enable people to become more self-sufficient in information access. This idea has also been expanded to indicate a possible advantage for reference departments. If people have a rudimentary grasp of library-use, it will relieve us of considerable drudgery.

Both of these ideas rest on the assumption that no one is better qualified to teach library-use than a librarian. This is where the rub has come in the profession. Several articulate opponents have argued that librarians are not teachers—they are information providers. If finding information for people is our real function then teaching might detract from our ability to do the best possible job of what we really should be doing.[2]

Furthermore, users might not want to know how to use the library, they might just want the information itself. It is even more of a failure on our part to try to teach someone who just wants direct information service. Some have argued that it is a mistaken notion that we can even succeed in library-use instruction—really effective library use is sophisticated and our real role is that of mediator and facilitator.[3] It has been argued that library-use instruction is necessarily a more conservative form of reference service, and that it held higher favor among earlier reference theorists is a misreading of those earlier theorists, and a misunderstanding of the relative roles of instruction and direct provision of information in reference service.[4]

Meanwhile, study after study confirms the fact that students respond well to library-use instruction, they express a desire to have it, their effectiveness in using the library increases, and library use itself even goes up.[5] Thousands of libraries (mostly school and academic, but other types as well) have implemented library-use instruction and made it part of the duties of reference personnel. Thelma Freides has concluded that, as far as academic libraries are concerned, the advocates of library-use instruction are dominant.[6] But its popularity has certainly not overshadowed all controversy.

ONLINE SEARCHING

Probably the next most popular topic in the literature of reference services is online searching. This developed in the 1970's and during the last few years has started to dominate the literature. It is a different kind of issue from library-use instruction because the demand for online searching is unavoidable. The information industry produces several new electronic databases every month. The volume of use of online services is constantly increasing. Many librarians resist promoting their online searching service for fear they will be deluged with requests beyond their ability to handle them. But for a reference department which claims to support information access and research not to at least offer online searching is becoming sheer folly. There are, however, several issues and controversies concerning online searching which deserve consideration.

The most debated issue in online searching among librarians is the fee or free issue. It has been intensified by the fact that in most libraries it is virtually impossible to implement free online searching without drawing budget away from collection development and other services. Not to have fees robs Peter to pay Paul. However, the primary argument against fees is that online databases will become more and more necessary to conduct standard reference work. Already, we see ready reference sources, encyclopedias, statistical databases, and cumulated runs of indexes, bibliographies, and catalogs appear in online form. It's difficult to justify charging fees for something which is part of basic reference service.[7] It will become increasingly cost effective and inevitable that reference work will rely on these sources. In one recent survey, it was discovered that a majority of newly implemented online services were offered free.[8]

Another issue is whether online searching should be integrated into the reference department or a separate related function. To integrate poses personnel and staffing problems. Training all or many reference professionals in online searching is expensive. Who searches and who does the more traditional reference work? If online searching is fully integrated into reference work will this increase the demand for expensive online searching beyond our ability to handle?

Not to integrate poses problems which are perhaps even more vexing. In special, research, and academic libraries more of our clientele are asking us for online services apart from any other reference work. And some library users are even starting to search on their own—without mediation, notably in chemistry, medicine, psychology and engineering. Thought provoking statements from faculty in universities include: "Did you know that the library still subscribes to a whole bunch of expensive indexes which I can easily and quickly search from my own desk—and I can store the results of my search, make bibliographies—the sky's the limit;" "Why should I go to the library? I just send my T.A. over to check out the source documents I want." It has been true for some time that many of our users see libraries only as institutions that store and circulate books, journals, and other materials. Consciously or unconsciously, there is an assumption that pretty much all we do is document delivery. But in the online age, if users can do *some* reference work—even ready reference work without help from the reference department, they will perhaps never discover any of the additional ways reference departments could help them (either with a specific topic or in general). Of course there is also a question of how well users can do online searching without help from reference professionals. Vocabulary control, choice of database, precision and recall of search results are all factors which benefit from an information professional's attention. Indeed, it is not difficult to support the contention that there is a huge gulf between what users do in practice and what really *should* be done—not only with online searching but with information gathering in general. Where does this leave reference services? It can be effectively argued that if reference departments don't incorporate and integrate online database searching, then users will simply begin to do it in some other way—and make even less effective use of reference services than before.

Another interesting trend is that these two most prominent topics of reference service: online searching and bibliographic instruction are, in a sense, pitted against each other. Online searching (as it is often practiced) encourages the avoidance of use of the library except for document delivery. Either the research is done by the librarian or by the client on the computer. It can appear that there would thus be a dwindling need for a knowledge of library use. Library instruction advocates respond that online searching is one more aspect of the library-use spectrum—one more resource that we should teach about.[9] It should be noted, however, that the goal of online searching is basically to obtain a bibliography on a topic. Library-use instruction should involve much more than producing a bibliography on a topic—it should involve methodology for topic selection, organizational and outline skills, bibliographic style, the structure of the entire literature—whether electronic or not, and the procedures for research. In fact, electronic information suggests a possible benefit to the calling of bibliographic instruction. It can provide a clerical function removing a lot of the drudgery of library-use and enable us to concentrate on a broader, more sophisticated understanding of how information should be gathered and how research should be done.

SPECIAL REFERENCE SERVICES

Some other very important developments during the last decade or two which have had significant impact on reference services can be grouped under the heading of special reference services. This category includes such things as I & R services, SDI services, services to the handicapped, custom reference or research services, information brokering, outreach services and community information services.

The questions that usually arise when considering such services are these: If we offer this service, can we really do a good job of it? Will doing this detract from our normal ongoing reference work and assisting people to use the library? Is it within our basic role and function to offer this service? In answering these and other questions, it should be noted that I & R services, services to the handicapped, various outreach programs, and some community information services have had wide acceptance. Many special libraries have been able to offer SDI services, custom research services, and various high-powered individualized special services.

One recent notion in the literature is that certain special services in reference departments stem from "a misguided philanthropic notion on the part of libraries" and an erroneous feeling that librarians should do more than just provide access to information.[10] After all, we are not really qualified to be counselors, social workers, diagnosticians, etc. It is the opinion of the authors that the services selected for inclusion here do conform to the customary role of librarian—information organizer, provider, and disseminator.

One special service that is interesting is the university based community information service. The prototypical example of this is called PENNTAP—Pennsylvania Technical Assistance Program at Penn State. Many other state universities have implemented or are considering similar programs. Basically it is a program whereby the reference department and a full-time staff of technical experts field questions from all over the commonwealth of Pennsylvania. The PENNTAP staff also disseminates critical scientific or technical information to needy users who may not have even requested it.[11] Some such programs are located in the university reference department while others just use the library as one source of possible answers. In any case, the entire university faculty is also available as a source of answers—and is therefore harnessed on behalf of the state taxpayer in solving problems. Most such services are free of charge.

STANDARDS AND GUIDELINES

Another ongoing issue in the reference literature is that of standards and guidelines. Since the RASD guidelines were adopted in 1976 and the ethics section was added in 1979, the main issue in the literature seems to be whether or not we can and should have quantitative standards. The RASD has also been working on standards for online searching. One important aspect of the standards is the requirement of a service policy manual in each reference program.[12] This seems to be a recommendation that is uniformly understood and accepted or even applauded in the literature—but not at all consistently done in practice.

There are various questions of ethics that continue to occupy the literature. Should the librarian recommend purchase of given titles?—in other words, endorse specific products? Should librarians give advice? Should the personal views of librarians enter the process at all?[13] Should the librarian help someone build a bomb by providing the information—or help someone commit suicide? Should librarians help runaways get married or criminals to find loopholes in the law? What circuitous information access methods are morally or ethically appropriate? The RASD statement of commitment—section 6 provides guidance on most of these questions[14] and most of the current literature seems to accept these ethical standards.

THE IMPACT OF TECHNICAL SERVICES ON REFERENCE SERVICES

The impact of automated library operations on the reference function has drawn much interest recently. Of key importance is the role reference departments must play in online public access catalogs.[15] The responsibility for user awareness and training falls on the reference department. Public relations, user resistance, terminal placement and in fact, the very design of the system and its software ultimately come to roost in the reference department. One example of this impact is seen in the fact that several libraries have implemented online catalogs with only a portion of the total collection in machine readable form. The remainder of the collection is then still available through the card catalog. Research on subject access with such catalogs indicates that users will often consult one form of the catalog—not both.[16] While partial conversion may be expedient from the technical services perspective, from the reference perspective, it may result in providing only partial access to the library's collection for many users. This is a very serious problem and one that deserves considerable attention.

Another interesting aspect of the automation explosion is affecting reference departments—microcomputers. Records management functions in reference departments that are very well suited to the microcomputer include vertical file maintenance, ILL record control, I & R files, word processing, local or special purpose indexes, use statistics, personnel scheduling, and pathfinder databases to name a few.[17]

Several libraries have provided public access to bibliographic utilities such as OCLC, RLIN, or WLN in the reference department. Patrons can do research, verification, or known item searching, and even local catalog access through these systems.[18]

RESOURCE SHARING

Always present in the literature is the issue of resource sharing and networking. The literature has taken on an increasingly negative complexion regarding resource sharing in the last few years. Some writers on the subject postulate that, in the final analysis, it is cheaper to buy most requested materials than to locate and borrow them from another library. But also in the literature are many continuing reports of successful cooperation. Many of the large academic and research libraries have increased their commitment to resource sharing—especially through the bibliographic utilities. RLIN, WLN, and LC have developed a basis for linking their authority files and bibliographic records.[19] Most of the states have made progress in developing union catalogs, serials lists, resource sharing arrangements, and automation networks.

Much of the progress, however, relates to document delivery rather than information access. Cooperative reference service providing actual search and discovery of information (including but not limited to bibliographic verification) continues to be practiced in many states and regions.[20] Networks like RLIN, OCLC and WLN, along with online searching are good reasons for optimism about cooperative information service, as machine readability certainly expedites cooperation. However, although the Library of Congress has worked with the state libraries in question referral, the problems of jurisdiction and type of library differences as well as funding have prevented anything resembling the national implementation of a patron's right to access to information beyond his or her own library. The RASD Cooperative Reference Service Committee is presently pretesting a form for communicating information requests from one library to another.[21]

There are many continuing controversies that relate to reference service that we can only mention here. For example, should there be a separate children's reference department in a public library, or one reference service? Should there be a separate undergraduate reference service in college and university libraries? How open or closed should reference collections be not only for access but for circulation? Should continuing education be the responsibility of the library or institution or is it the responsibility of the individual? Should non-professionals work at the reference desk and, if so, to what extent? How should reference departments be managed—and how should managers be developed or selected? The list can go on and on.

PROFESSIONALISM

But let us move on to what will be the last topic of discussion and what is among the most important of all the issues presented so far. It can be called the issue of professionalism. It can also be identified as a topic which has not been as popular as most of the above subjects in terms of volume of published pages but it has had sporadic and continuing attention for many years—really throughout most of the history of our profession. What is reference work? Writers like Wynar, Vavrek, Whittaker, Rettig, Katz and others have all grappled with this question.[22] Most of the controversies mentioned above come back to this question: just what is reference work, and what is a professional librarian?

Recently the Office of Personnel Management (OPM) lowered the civil service classification of librarians in federal libraries so that people without MLS degrees can qualify to obtain these positions. The Office of Management and Budget (OMB) has adopted a new policy demanding that information services and research be contracted out to the private sector rather than performed by government libraries, information centers, and other agencies.[23] Also recently, Mississippi State University was sued by Glenda Merwine over the question, does a university have a right to require an MLS degree as a condition for employment? The case is still in litigation but ALA has decided not to be involved at this time.[24]

It appears that librarianship is in a bit of an identity crisis. In the May 1984 issue of *American Libraries*, there is an article which basically asserts that current reference practice is in a state of great confusion and turmoil—certainly very much part of the same identity crisis.[25] Much of the author's concern is tied in with the fact that we are doing more than ever before—so much more that we may not be able to continue doing it well—we're on a tread mill. Unfortunately, there are other writers who have voiced similar feelings of "sturm und drang." Quite recently, Bernard Vavrek asserted that not only is the golden age of reference librarianship over but concern must now be voiced about the future of librarianship itself as a viable function in a modern society.[26]

What is the answer to this conundrum? Perhaps if we balance our efforts towards document delivery with provision of information (making better use of our literature reviewing skills and our knowledge of information transfer in the various disciplines and areas of interest) we will be more credible in our insistence on rigorous educational and professional standards for those who provide such service.

Are we, indeed, professionals? Let us follow the lead of Pauline Wilson. In an article in September, 1984 *American Libraries* on the Merwine Case and OPM decisions, she says simply that we have used the professional model about which to organize our work for several decades.[27] We may not be a perfect profession, but by our own choices we fit that model better than we do others. Given the variety of trends and controversies, how should a professional reference librarian act? One of the chief features of a profession is that the practitioner takes responsibility for some portion of a client's welfare. For the moment we will avoid such issues as the preparation, body of knowledge, and other aspects of a profession which give the professional the needed expertise, and emphasize simply that as professional reference librarians we take responsibility for the information welfare of a client. This is crucial. We do not provide reference service for the sake of being nice to the patron, or to make the patron feel good. We do not provide good reference service by telling the patron what we happen to know, or by telling the patron what we can readily find. Rather, we take responsibility for the information welfare of the patron. This requires an active rather than defensive stance. It does not mean we are slaves, any more than other professionals are slaves. If we cannot help the patron because the information need has been brought to us too late, we need to level with the patron, just as a lawyer may have to tell a client—why didn't you ask me before you engaged in such and such behavior, or entered a flawed contract. The long term information welfare of the patron may be best served by calling attention to what the patron needs to do this time or next time to be better informed. That may include some version of the directive—next time bring me a better question. The most important element, here, though is that we have accepted a responsibility.

Another characteristic of a professional is the dominance of conscious activity, based on training, reading, study and research. To put it bluntly, too often we operate on automatic. Just as one can identify doctors, nurses and other individual practitioners who have not kept up to date, who are not "professionally alive" so are there reference librarians who somehow think they can just show up at the desk for another day of work and all will be well. All will not be well. There are new sources to be learned, new developments in society and in various disciplines, erosion of interpersonal skills once held, and other factors that only conscious action can remedy. We must take this responsibility.

As one thinks about acquaintances in various professions, are they not often individuals who are both plugged into local events and activities, and at the same time, more so than most people in the community, tuned into the outside world? Should this not also be the case with the reference librarian, to assure that the library is the window to the larger world for those who wish to use it as such? Notwithstanding the Planning Process' attention to interests within the community, the library, and its reference service should provide access to a wider base of information and materials.

The next aspect of professionalism has to do with the fact that the professional operates in a transparent way in regard to other professionals in the same field—the work of the individual professional is subject in some way to scrutiny by others. This is much talked about in medicine, and ethical committees exist in the legal profession to oversee behavior of the individual lawyer. Yet why do we resist oversight of our own reference work? Among the extensive literature on measurement and evaluation of reference service one usually finds the notion that such activities are for improvement of service generally, and should not be used to evaluate the individual reference librarian. It seems to us we should expect to have our work evaluated—the more reference encounters that can be evaluated and in other ways shared by and with our colleagues, the better will be our service. The acceptance of such scrutiny would indeed be good evidence of the acceptance of responsibility for the information welfare of the patron as mentioned above. The true professional communicates in many ways with colleagues and accepts the scrutiny of peers.

Another aspect of professionalism is the responsibility to protect the resources of the profession so that it can meet its responsibilities. It is not enough to wring our hands and say "We can't take responsibility for our patron's information welfare. We lost two lines on the budget last year." We must see that the resources are there. Do we stand by idly while they are eroded, even to provide other services within and without the library? Do we know where we stand in reference service in comparison to five years ago as far as resources go? It would be interesting to see data across the country on that subject.

Another aspect of professionalism is that of personal quality control. Are you the reference librarian you used to be, or have you become something less than you were, or less than you hoped to become? It seems common to find in our students the opinion that things must be getting better in reference librarianship, that recent graduates don't evidence the forbidding tone that they recall in contacts with "old time" librarians. It is our contention that we are susceptible to becoming reflections of our worst fears, or that of which we are most critical. Only through discipline (professionalism) will we be otherwise—and we owe it to ourselves and to our profession to exercise that discipline.

Perhaps it is true that we cannot espouse sound theory on the nature of reference work. Without well developed theory, a well ordered philosophy of reference service is impossible to articulate. Perhaps this is just because of one major, unavoidable, yet truly exciting fact—reference service, in the end, is passive in the best sense of the word. While we will prepare ourselves well, discipline ourselves to provide the best possible services at all times based on the best available resources, we will do so to topics and information needs brought to us by our patrons. Until we receive an individual request, we cannot fully anticipate its nature, and we should so construct our services to best react to the ideosyncratic nature of the next, unknown request.

But there are some things we can anticipate, and as a profession we have attempted to do so in an official document—the RASD Commitment to Reference Service Guidelines, mentioned above. How well are these known? Do we care about what they say? Are we ready to dismiss guidelines we can't reach as unfeasible or idealistic? The Guidelines say that you must have a professional reference librarian on duty at all times that the library is open. Is that so outlandish? It is if we see the sine qua non of library service as document delivery or provision of study hall space. But if we believe a library to be more than that—if we believe that as a profession we take responsibility for our patrons' information welfare, it doesn't sound so outlandish. There are many further examples of important policy issues spoken to in this document. We suggest that a good start to a renewed dedication to reference service would be a reading of these guidelines, a commitment to their implementation, and attention to revisions as they occur.

Even if we act as professionals, accepting responsibility, are disciplined in behavior, and attentive to standards, there are still great dilemmas. Prime among these is the boundary of service. What information is appropriate for us to get for patrons—anything? Certainly not. "What's my Uncle Ted doing next Friday?" That question is unanswerable, and it is information, but few libraries would seek the answer. The definition with which this paper opens attempts to ward off this dilemma by stating that we are involved with information that is in some way connected to the graphic record of mankind. This seems somewhat too limiting. Although we cannot solve this dilemma here, it is best to keep the definition as broad as possible, not using false niceties to limit it, such as we often do with medical or legal questions. "Won't I get sued?" Let me quote L.S. Allen in a book on consumer health information: "As far as anyone has been able to determine from reported legal decisions, no librarian has ever been held liable for damages for negligence in supplying or failing to supply information to a patron."[28] In other words, worry about lawsuits and other such worries may mask unwillingness to provide the service we should be providing.

In conclusion, let us emphasize individual and collective professional responsibility. This includes the responsibility not to accept blindly what is put forth here. It should be questioned. One should consciously arrive at defensible professional standards. Only then will we become the professionals we can and want to become.

REFERENCES

1. Thelma Freides, "Current Trends in Academic Libraries," *Library Trends* 31(Winter 1983): 458-59.
2. See summary of arguments and discussion by James Rice, "Library-Use Instruction with Individual Users: Should Instruction Be Included in the Reference Interview?" *Reference Librarian* 10(Spring/Summer 1984): 75-77.
3. See summary of arguments and discussion by William A. Katz, Introduction Reference Work, 2 vols. 4th ed. (New York: McGraw Hill, 1982), vol 2: *Reference Services and Reference Processes*, p. 59.
4. Robert Wagers, "American Reference Theory and the Information Dogma," *Journal of Library History* 13(Summer 1978): 265-81.
5. See the following for a fairly complete list: Arthur P. Young, "Research on Library-

User Education: A Review Essay," in *Educating the Library User*, ed. John Lubans, Jr. (New York: Bowker, 1984), pp. 1-15. Arthur P. Young and Exir B. Brennan,"Bibliographic Instruction: A Review of Research and Applications," in *Progress in Educating the Library User*, ed. John Lubans, Jr. (New York: Bowker, 1978), pp. 13-28. Deborah L. Lockwood, *Library Instruction: A Bibliography* (Westport, Connecticut: Greenwood, 1979). Hannelore B. Rader, "Library Orientation and Instruction. . . ," *Reference Services Review* 9(April 1981): 79-89; 10(Summer 1982): 33-41; 11(Summer 1983): 57-65; 12(Summer 1984): 59-71.

6. Freides, "Current Trends," p. 459.

7. James Rice, "Fees for Online Searches: A Review of the Issue and a Discussion of Alternatives," *Journal of Library Administration* 3(Spring 1982): 25-33.

8. Mary Jo Lynch, *Financing Online Services in Publicly Supported Libraries: The Report of an ALA Survey* (Chicago: American Library Association, 1981). See *RQ* 21(Spring 1982): 223-26 for a summary.

9. Freides, "Current Trends," p. 466.

10. David Isaacson, "Library Inreach," *RQ* 23(Fall 1983): 65.

11. For information, contact PENNTAP (Pennsylvania Technical Assistance Program), J. Orvis Keller Building, University Park, Pennsylvania 16802.

12. A Commitment to Information Services: Developmental Guidelines 1979," *RQ* 19(Spring 1979): 277-78.

13. Mary Prokop and Charles McClure, "The Public Librarian and Service Ethics: A Dilemma," *Public Library Quarterly* 3(Winter 1982): 69-81.

14. "A Commitment to Information Services," p. 277.

15. P. K. Swanson, "Reference Librarians and Online Catalogs," *RQ* 23(Fall 1983): 23-26.

16. Joseph Matthews, ed., *Using Online Catalogs: A Nationwide Survey* (New York: Neal Schuman, 1983), p. 85.

17. N. C. Jacobson and Natalie Slurr, "Automated Reference Desk: Three Ways Libraries Can Use Computers to Enhance Reference Services," *American Libraries* 15(May 1984): 324.

18. J. E. Miller, "OCLC and RLIN as Reference Tools," *Sound of Academic Librarianship* 8(November 1982): 270-77. Swanson, "Reference Librarians," pp. 23-26. S. C. Farmer, "RLIN As a Reference Tool," *Online* 6(September 1982): 14-22. Kathleen Low, "RLIN and WLN Databases: Not for Catalogers Only," *American Libraries* 15(May 1984): 326.

19. Ray Denenberg and Sally McCallum, RLG/WLN/LC Computers Ready to Talk," *American Libraries* 15(June 1984): 400-4.

20. For bibliography on the cooperative reference attempts see Marjorie E. Murfin and Lubomyr R. Wynar, eds. *Reference Service An Annotated Bibliographic Guide* (Littleton, Colorado: Libraries Unlimited, 1977), pp. 214-222 and Supplement (1984), pp. 221-25.

21. A copy of this Information Request Form may be obtained by sending a self addressed #10 envelope to The Reference and Adult Services Division, American Library Association, 50 East Huron, Chicago, Illinois 60611.

22. Bohdan Wynar, "Reference Theory: Situation Hopeless But Not Impossible," *College and Research Libraries* 28(September 1967): 337- 42. Bernard Vavrek, "A Theory of Reference Service," *College and Research Libraries* 29(November 1968): 508-510. Ken Whittaker, "Toward A Theory of Reference and Information Service," *Journal of Librarianship* 9(January 1977): 49-63. James Rettig, "A Theoretical Model and Definition of the Reference Process," *RQ* 18(Fall 1978): 19-29. Bill Katz, "The Uncertain Realities of Reference Service," *Library Trends* 31(Winter 1983): 363-374.

23. "Public vs. Private Sector," *The Bowker Annual of Library and Book Trade Information: 1984*, Julia Ehresmann ed. (New York: Bowker, 1984), pp. 6-7.

24. Edward G. Holley, "The Merwine Case and the MLS: Where Was ALA?" *American Libraries* 15(May 1984): 327-331. Reader Forum—"More on Merwine, Holley and the MLS," *American Libraries* 15(July/August 1984): 482-85. Robert Wedgeworth,

"ALA and the Merwine Case: A Word as to the WHYS," *American Libraries* 15(September 1984): 561-62.

25. William Miller, "What's Wrong with Reference?" *American Libraries* 15(May 1984): 303-06; 321-22.

26. Bernard Vavrek, Introduction to issue, "Current Trends in Reference Services," *Library Trends* 31(Winter, 1983): 361.

27. Pauline Wilson, "ALA, the MLS, and Professional Employment: An Observers Field Guide to the Issues," *American Libraries* 15(September 1984): 563-66.

28. Luella S. Allen, "Legal and Ethical Considerations in Providing Health Information," in *Developing Consumer Health Information Services*, ed. Alan M. Rees (New York: Bowker, 1982), p. 45.

WHO WILL WORK THE PUBLIC SERVICE DESKS?

Selecting, Training and Retaining Staff for the Library's Public Service Desks

Carol Lee Anderson

Much has been written about staffing the library's reference desk and providing reference service to library users. However, it is often forgotten that in many libraries, there are other public assistance points in addition to the reference desk. Smaller libraries may have only one public assistance desk—circulation—which also provides any reference or information services required by patrons.

Although many patrons who enter a library building use the services of the reference desk, many patrons never approach the library's reference desk. A number of patrons form their opinions of the quality of library service solely based on their experiences at the library's other public service desks. Thus, for a library interested in excellent overall service, staff at the other public service desks must be able to provide at least a minimal level of informational or "reference" assistance.

How, then do these other service points complement services offered by the library's reference desk? The key is the staff working on these other desks. The following discussion suggests methods for selecting staff, establishing an initial training program, retaining staff, scheduling staff and planning an on-going training program. At a basic level, the persons staffing public service desks outside of reference provide directional and informational assistance about the building and services. At a more sophisticated level, the staff should recognize a reference question so patrons are referred to the appropriate person or area for the required information. At the highest level, the staff provide the required information or assist the patron in locating the information. This "highest level" is best illustrated by a microform collections staff—often they best know collection

---

Ms. Anderson is Assistant Director, Access Services, University Libraries, State University of New York, Albany, NY 12222.

© 1986 by The Haworth Press, Inc. All rights reserved.

contents because finding aids to microform collections are notoriously inadequate. In some ways, a good microforms staff is akin to a good staff in the library's manuscript collection—both acquire knowledge of the collection through working with it and processing it. A staff member's knowledge becomes the real "finding tool" for accessing the information contained in the collection.

This article provides information for librarians who supervise public service desks in the larger academic libraries. "Public service desk" is the term used throughout to denote the circulation, reserve and microforms desks as well as desks serving periodicals collections or those set up to serve a specific physical area of the library. This article should also benefit librarians who work on the library's reference desk since the reference librarians often forget the level of informational activity taking place at the other public service desks.

SELECTING STAFF FOR THE SERVICE DESK

In an academic library, many of the public service desks are staffed primarily by part-time employees and in most cases the part-timers are students at the college or university. The ideal staffing pattern is always having the same, well-trained full time employees assigned to work at the service desk. Lack of enough full time staff positions coupled with the number of hours per week that the desk must be staffed are factors mitigating against the "ideal." Thus, time and care must be given to recruiting and selecting the part time clerical staff as well as the full time clerical staff.

Make sure that the people staffing the service desk *want* to be there! Staff who do not like dealing with the public will cause numerous image problems for the library. Also, a match between staff skills and position requirements is a must. A staff member may greatly enjoy working with patrons but happens to be a real klutz with equipment. While this individual may work out well at the reserve desk that uses a manual circulation system, the same person will be an absolute disaster in the microforms area when he or she has to load a new roll of paper into the reader-printer.

How does an interviewer find out if a potential employee is suited for the position? First, develop a position description. The position description sets forth the supervisor's expectations for the position. The position description is necessary for the prospective candidates as well. Perhaps after reviewing the position description, a potential candidate may decide not to apply for the position, saving time for both the potential candidate and the interviewer.

Prior to interviewing a candidate, try to review his or her application or resume in advance. The preparatory work makes the interview go much more smoothly. Note down specific items or points on which more information would be helpful and use these notes when conducting the interview.

At the interview, the candidate needs to be put at ease. Start off with a non-job related inquiry to make him or her a little more relaxed. Move into the body of the interview using the resume or application. Ask the candidate to describe position duties at the last job. What did the person like most about the job? What did the person like least? Why did the person leave or why does the person want to leave? Ask these same questions for all positions previously held by the candidate.

Get the interviewee talking. Do not make the mistake made by so many interviewers: the interviewer does all the talking, explaining what is wanted. When this happens clever interviewees know just what to say in order to be the "successful" candidate. After all, the interviewer *gave* the candidate all the "right" answers.

After the supervisor has posed questions to the candidate, ask the candidate if he or she has any questions. The candidate's response at this point assists the supervisor in gauging the candidate's interest in the position and enthusiasm (or lack thereof) for the position.

For the supervisor who is unsure of his or her interviewing skills, he or she will want to do some further reading on interviewing techniques.[1] Perhaps interviewing workshops are offered locally or, arrange an interviewing workshop for all library supervisors. The university's business school or personnel office are good sources for workshop leaders.

Always check the applicants' references regardless of the position.[2] Keep notes when checking references. Devising a telephone reference form often saves steps. By using a form, the interviewer is sure that he or she has consistently checked references, asking the same questions of each reference. Questions to ask include: would the former supervisor rehire the person—why or why not? What are the individual's strengths and weaknesses? What was the individual's position and what were the job duties? With the last question, the supervisor cross checks information supplied by the candidate.

Clues from the candidate and from the references assist the supervisor in the selection process. Assemble the information on each candidate, including the application or resume plus the references or reference notes. After reviewing all information, sometimes the selection decision is fairly easy. Perhaps a candidate said she disliked dealing with rude customers at a previous sales clerking position. This is a clue that she may not enjoy working at the circulation desk. Another candidate may have said his previous position was wonderful except for the typing assignments. The supervisor knows that this person will not cheerfully undertake typing of reserve slips. Having two or more strong candidates in the pool puts the supervisor in a fortunate position. With several strong candidates, the person most closely matching the job description and organizational outlook is selected.

The interview process and checking of references is a time consuming process. The supervisor or interviewer must view this as an investment. It is better to take a little extra time in making a good selection than to select an inappropriate person. If not enough time is expended and decisions are made hurriedly, an incorrect "match" may result. The supervisor then spends time and endless energy trying to correct, modify or retrain an individual who is not right for the position.

College work-study students can pose a problem, especially when the library does not have any control over which students are assigned to the library. Working closely with the institutional financial aid office is highly desirable when the library is dependent on college work study help. Build and maintain a good working relationship with the financial aid office and this will pay dividends. The office needs a very good idea of the positions needing to be filled and the qualifications sought. Provide copies of the job descriptions for a good start with the financial aid office.

INITIAL TRAINING

All staff must have an idea of where all basic services and functions are located in the building so each staff member is able to answer directional questions. Patrons are understandably irritated if sent to the third floor when what they needed was only steps away. New staff also must realize how their particular service or activity fits into the larger library picture.

If the library has developed an introductory audio visual presentation for new patrons, the first component of the staff training program is built around this. A self guided tour, developed for patrons, is also useful when training new staff. After all, staff should at least know the same information disseminated to the general public. In other words, look for general training tools that have been developed.

If a self guided tour is not available, then a walking tour conducted by the supervisor is a must. If a self guided tour is available, a supervisor's tour is a helpful addition. New staff have the opportunity to ask the questions not answered in the printed tour and the supervisor assesses the new staff members' knowledge of the library. The tour assists the supervisor and new employee in the establishment of their working relationship.

Make new staff aware of flyers, brochures and general informational guides about the library and its services. In fact, a collection of these materials should be housed in a binder at each public service desk. If staff do not know where the water fountains are located or which office sets up appointments for a computer search, then they should know where to find that information.

After the "general" training about the library, the new staff member is trained in his or her position duties. This component of the training may take a couple of weeks as staff learn how to shelve, work on the service desk or perform other duties and responsibilities of the position. During this portion of the training, staff learn about the tools and guides available for providing assistance in their particular areas. For a periodicals collection, they need to know about all the guides or printouts and also the limitations of these tools. At the reserve desk, they need to know the overall policies which govern the operation. Again, collect the flyers, policies and guides and place them in one location at each service desk so they are quickly available when staff need to look up or verify information.

The third component of training is the instruction on recognizing a reference question and making the appropriate referrals. Start by asking the head of reference to conduct a tour of the library's reference collection. Staff need an idea of what is contained in the reference collection plus examples of typical reference questions. Show staff how major sources are utilized. Where relevant, the tour should also include information about the tools used to access the collection in the new staff member's public service area. For periodicals desk staff, for example, the various guides to the periodical literature need to be pointed out. Access tools developed by the library need to be described—is the card catalog the authority on all serials titles or does the library have a serials catalog? Does a printout duplicate the catalogs? Is the printout an imperfect "duplication"? Staff servicing the microforms collection need to understand the various controls—or lack of controls—over the collections. Are the monograph collections on microformat analyzed in the card catalog or on-line catalog? Are the serials on microformat in the library's serials printout or in the serials catalog? If not, what access tools *are* available?

After touring the reference collection, assign staff to "observe" at the reference desk for an hour. New staff acquire a feel for what the reference staff do, recognize the nature of reference questions and acquire a broader knowledge of the library. Follow up this exercise with a discussion with the new employee. At this point the supervisor emphasizes that the public service desk does not replace the reference desk staff in answering questions. The occasions when referrals are made to the reference desk is a concept emphasized at this time.

Devise and assign practice questions for all three components of the training. This should be fairly easy to do since a trainer can jot down commonly asked questions at that particular service desk. Use these same questions or another set of questions at the end of training as an informal test to see if the new staff member has learned and retained what is considered necessary to perform job duties.

By the end of the training, a staff member should not have to say "I don't know" in response to an inquiry. The response is "I'll check on that" or "please go to the reference desk, located in the east wing, for that information." When staff do not know the answer, they should know who *will* know and thus, a large portion of their assistance may well consist of referrals—whether to their supervisor or to another office or service area.

Telephone skills are often overlooked when planning a training program. How is a staff member supposed to answer the phone—what identifying information is to be imparted after picking up the receiver? What information is required when a caller leaves a message? The standard telephone message forms are of great assistance, helping staff to gather all relevant information: date and time of call; who took the message; who called for whom; and the message. If the staff member requested is not available, does the person answering the phone offer assistance? Does the person answering the phone say that the person is away from his or her desk or does he or she say "John Doe will call you when he returns from the staff party."

With student employees, many may not have had previous work experience. In this instance, the supervisor is not only training the individual for working in the library but the supervisor is also teaching the student good work habits. The students need to understand their responsibilities in maintaining their work schedules, demonstrate their dependability as members of a team and realize that they project an image of the employer.

ON-GOING TRAINING

Once staff have the basic skills required to work their public service desk, take steps to build upon these basic skills. Use regular work assignments as well as in-service training programs to do this.

Although not usually considered an integral part of on-going training, "regular" work assignments contribute vastly to an employee's knowledge of the service desk and the collections served in this area of the library. Staff and supervisors do not realize the extent of knowledge about the service desk or the collection, accumulated in the work process. Reshelving or refiling materials helps staff learn what the collection contains and what is used by the patrons. Conducting collection inventories is another way staff learn about collections contents and usage. Pulling journals for binding or discarding newspapers received on microfilm are also important tasks for the same reasons.

Assignments for writing or updating collection guides also help staff increase their knowledge of collection contents. In the process of writing entries for a guide to the microform collections and double checking information for the guide, the staff member learns collection contents. The completed guide is useful at both the microforms and reference desks, adding another dimension to collection access.

Developing and updating other guides or handouts used by the public and staff provides growth opportunities for that individual to work on his or her writing skills. In the process of collecting, writing, editing and verifying information for the guides, a staff member also learns more about those segments of the collection.

Staff tend to specialize in their position duties. From a motivational standpoint, there is much to be said for giving someone a task at which he or she excels. However, consider rotating assignments among various public service desks so each staff member has an opportunity to learn about the other parts of the library. Rotations enhance their ability to provide accurate information to patrons.

In-service training programs are a more formalized method of providing on-going training. Special talks or lectures prepared about the particular collections or services are a traditional means for keeping staff up-to-date and building on their existing knowledge and skills. The staff member who prepares the talk acquires more knowledge of the operation in the process of preparing the presentation and then shares that knowledge with others.

Visiting speakers who conduct specific workshops are another option for in-service training presentations. Vendors of some products or services are more than willing to provide speakers, slide-tapes, or other tools about their products.

Never underestimate the value of special, in-depth tours of other library operations. The more staff know about the library and the services, the more effective they become. Staff should have tours of collections, services or operations closely connected with the area where they work. Persons working the periodicals desk will benefit if they know the serials acquisitions process, for example. During initial training, circulation desk staff probably did not have time to visit any of the library's special collections. Arrange tours for these staff members. The quality of their directional assistance will increase.

If the supervisor plans to modify operations or procedures, arrange visits to other similar libraries. The visit not only builds staff knowledge of other similar collections and operations, but staff view their operation in a different and hopefully more analytical way. Information gathered on these visits helps staff seek group solutions for the potential changes in the operations.

RETAINING STAFF

Once staff members are recruited, trained, and have worked within a certain set of position duties for awhile, they may become bored with what they are doing. When boredom sets in, the quality of work performance slides, a poor image of the service is presented, the individual is eventually "lost" to the organization.

Recruitment and training are expensive processes since much staff time is consumed if doing both functions well. After investing in the effectiveness of each staff member, take time to plan how to retain these now well-trained individuals. Retaining staff is the best way to maximize the interviewing and training investment. Take steps to help staff *before* boredom sets in.[3]

Look at the various functions performed at the service desk. Is it possible to create promotional opportunities? Give the staff goals or steps for which to strive. Consider starting all part-time staff with shelving or refiling of materials. In the process of shelving, they learn how to use call numbers, learn locations of various functions and services and also learn the working habits expected by the library. If successful with the shelving assignment, after a semester or two, they are eligible for "promotion" to working directly with the public on the service desk.

Some library operations have student supervisors, available hours when full time staff members are not available. This makes another "promotional opportunity" and again sets a goal for staff to strive towards.

Assigning a staff member responsibility for certain tasks or functions increases their sense of importance to the operation. They take pride in keeping a certain area or function up-to-date. Supervisors must be sure to recognize a job that has been done well.

Establishment of unit objectives as a group and then working as a team to accomplish these objectives makes each individual feel part of the group and share in a sense of accomplishment. Perhaps the objective is moving the public service desk, shifting the collection, implementing a new system or revising a procedure. At any rate, the accomplishments are tangible. When setting objectives, be sure they fit with the goals of the public service desk and the goals of the library.

Current staff should assist in training the new staff. Perhaps the title of "trainer" is another promotional opportunity for current staff. Exercise caution when selecting the trainers. New staff will pattern themselves after those already in place. From current staff, the new employee will pick up cues as to what is considered "acceptable" and what is considered "unacceptable." New staff will mimic the manner for answering telephone questions, for example.

Some libraries or institutions are able to create pay incentives. Staff who have been employed x consecutive semesters or years are paid an across-the-board increase or student supervisors are paid more. Ideally, increased pay rates should reward good work performance as well as longevity.

Office parties or staff social occasions are important ways to develop an *esprit de corps*. These are particularly important when the staff works a varied schedule. A social event may be the only time the Sunday staff sees the crew who works Thursdays. Parties are also ways to mark the completion of a particularly important task and a way to recognize everyone's hard work.

SCHEDULING

As previously mentioned, the ideal for each service desk is the availability of full time, well trained staff all hours of operation. Several approaches are possible for providing the best level of service for users.

Each staff member should know whom is his or her back-up person. One person in the area is always designated as being "in charge" to handle general referrals, emergencies, and patron complaints. The person in charge of the service area must know who is in charge of the library building so fine complaints, medical emergencies and the problem patrons are channeled in the proper directions. In the service desk's staff manual, a full list of referral names and phone numbers is a must.

Part-time staff are most effective if they work in shifts lasting at least two hours and work for a minimum of ten hours per week. Staff working shifts shorter than two hours in length barely get started before having to leave again. Numerous staff members working less than ten hours a week become a liability, requiring extensive scheduling because more people must be scheduled and then trained to cover the hours. Staff working less than ten hours per week also need constant re-training in the "basics."

If staff positions have eroded in recent years and it is harder and harder to maintain service desk hours, take a critical look at the operation. It is possible to reduce service desk hours by closing the area earlier or opening later? Look at available hourly data to determine the "busy times." Compare seating counts (how many seats occupied at a certain hour), building or room entrance counts (how many bodies came in), and usage of services at those hours. If these figures are not readily available, collect data on a sample basis for pre-selected time periods. The figures may well show that Reserve averages three loans between 11 and midnight and two seats out of 150 are occupied when the seat count is taken at 11:15 p.m. Taking samples throughout one semester is wise before making a final decision to modify hours.

NOT A REPLACEMENT FOR THE REFERENCE DESK

Staff members working the library's public service desks must be reminded on occasion that they do not replace reference services. This is easiest if the service area must refer patrons back to the reference area for use of the proper access tools. Formal visits to or observations at the reference desk every six months or so reinforce this concept. Other public service desk supervisors must maintain open lines of communication with the head of reference. By the same token, reinforce the role of the other public service desks with those staff members because these "non-reference" desks are a critical component in the library's services. After all, the other public service desks would not exist is they did not perform vital services to the public and to the library organization.

REFERENCES

1. The literature on interviewing and selection is extensive. The selections listed below present varying approaches to the interview process.

William T. Wolz recommends a structured interview using twelve questions. He also suggests appropriate and inappropriate responses to the questions in "How to Interview Supervisory Candidates from the Ranks." (*Personnel* 57 (September-October 1980): 31-39.)

"Selection Systems for Clerical Positions," authored by Dennis J. Kravetz, recommends interviews combined with testing as the most effective selection system. The article points out the importance of validating selection tests. (*Personnel Administrator* 26 (February 1981): 39-42.)

Thomas A. Petit and Terry W. Mullins propose a scale for scoring applicants based on job skills; compatibility between applicant's and interviewer's expectations; proper motivation; and desirable personal traits. The article is entitled "Decisions, Decisions: How to Make Good Ones on Employee Selection." (*Personnel* 58 (March-April 1981): 71-77.)

"How to Hire a Winner" by Philip R. Matheny (*Supervisory Management* 20 (May 1984): 12-15) outlines an eight step selection process starting with development of written position duties and ending with the checking of references. Excellent pointers are provided for each step.

Assessment through Interviewing by George Shouksmith (Oxford, England: Pergamon Press, 1978. Second Edition) addresses both individual and group interviewing techniques. *Interviewing for Managers: A Complete Guide to Employment Interviewing* by John D. Drake (New York: AMACOM, 1982. Revised Edition) includes a chapter on equal employment regulations. The Appendices are helpful.

2. A check of employment references can be accomplished a variety of ways. For more

information, start with Rawle Deland's "Reference Checking Methods" (*Personnel Journal* 62 (June 1983): 458-463.) Deland suggests the people whom should be contacted for references and then how to evaluate responses made by the references.

Fifteen questions to ask in a reference interview are listed in "The Delicate Art of Checking References." While geared towards checking of references for supervisors and managers, it is of value for all position levels. The article is by Paula Lippin and is in the August 1979 issue of *Administrative Management* (40), pages 30-32.

Reference reports are used by some agencies and firms. Although most academic recruiters do not utilize reference reports, the article by Paul M. Muchinsky, "Use of Reference Reports," (*Journal of Occupational Psychology* 52 (December 1979): 287-297) may be of general interest.

3. For those interested in reading more on employee retention and turnover, a number of monographs and articles are available. *Employee Turnover: Causes, Consequences, and Control* by William H. Mobley (Reading, Massachusetts: Addison-Wesley Publishing Company, 1982) provides an overview of the varous issues. *Job Enrichment for Results: Strategies for Successful Implementation* (by Roy W. Walters and Associates, Inc.; Reading, Massachusetts: Addison-Wesley Publishing Company, 1975) discusses the various approaches to motivation theory and then moves into discussing job enrichment programs. Case studies are included.

Choosing How to Staff the Reference Desk

John Montag

One of the more interesting staff room discussion topics, one rarely mentioned in the literature of librarianship, centers on the question of whether reference librarians are born or made. I remain ambivalent on the question. I nod sagely at whoever has the floor at the moment, and finally decide, like Solomon, that both views are right. As a former little leaguer and erstwhile slow-pitch player, I can assert with some authority that baseball players are born. As one whose three-year-old does a better job of coloring inside the lines I can make a similar assertion about artists. But as a fan and avid reader of both Roger Angell and Tom Boswell I am constantly reminded that ballplayers develop. They go to spring training; they work their way up through the minors; they practice constantly, both on the fundamentals and on the nuances of the game. Is Pete Rose naturally great or did he make himself that way? The question is not wholly frivolous, and applies to all artists, be they painters, sculptors, ballplayers, or reference librarians.

Talent alone is almost never enough. It calls for training, guidance, nurturing, and as in the old joke about the cabbie, who when asked about how to get to Carnegie Hall, replied: "Practice, practice, practice." After all, one "practices" an art; lawyers "practice" law; physicians have "practices." But how does one come to practice them? Through the apprentice system that gave rise to this particular use of the term "practice"? Or through the educational system of graduate and professional schools that stamp their imprimatur on those who have become socialized into the arcane mysteries that make up the profession's particular expertise?

This is the implication behind the question of the origins of reference librarians. Like the question, the implication is not wholly

---

The author is Director, Office of Information, State Library of Iowa, E. 12th & Grand, Des Moines, IA 50319.

© 1986 by The Haworth Press, Inc. All rights reserved.

frivolous. Reference librarians have to come from somewhere. But the way some people carry on about the use of paraprofessionals (i.e., those without the M.L.S.) at the reference desk, one would think that Chicken Little was right. They discuss such use of paraprofessionals in terms of the damage it does to the "professionalism" of librarians and in terms of the lowering of both the status and salary of the "professional." They miss the point.

LOCAL CHOICE

The profession does not exist merely to promote itself. Neither do libraries exist to provide salaries and status to their employees. A number of studies have established that paraprofessionals have performed and are able to perform a large number of tasks once considered professional. Mugnier's study, published by A.L.A., argues that given the way supervisors assign duties, none of "the tasks that involve readers' service to the public on a one-to-one basis . . . is exclusively a professional activity."[1] The important point then lies not in arguing whether paraprofessionals should be at the reference desk. That decision has already been made in the innumerable daily choices of supervisors who, facing budget constraints or ideology, practiced what one colleague calls "pragmatism run amuck" and what others call or imply is expediency.

We should not be side-tracked by the false issue of professional status. The real issue is always what is best for my library. The use of paraprofessionals is more than a global issue. It is a local issue. Local circumstances determine and should determine a library's response to the topic. Factors to be considered in making a well-thought out decision include: quality of service, personnel and personnel policies, training resources, equity, and budget. The overriding factor is quality of service, but that means different things in different contexts. Given the current state of knowledge, the following discussion must, like any such discussion, remain suggestive rather than definitive.

QUALITY OF SERVICE

Recent evaluations of the quality of answers given by the average library staff to reference questions is clearly unfavorable. Nevertheless, none of it justifiably argues against the use of paraprofessionals. The evidence of differences in the question-answering ability of librarians and paraprofessionals remains mixed. Bunge's study in the mid-sixties identified equal ability to provide accurate answers, but gave a slight, but significant edge to librarians in speed and efficiency.

Both Mugnier and St. Clair and Aluri[2] contend that paraprofessionals are capable of providing reference service. Neither, however, successfully answers the question of how well that service is performed. Mugnier bases her contention on a survey of and follow-up interviews of the "feelings" of supervisors toward paraprofessionals. In her interviews she found that although 20% of the supervisors felt that as a group graduate librarians at the first level performed better than paraprofessionals as a group, as many as 50% saw no difference in performance. This is hardly reassuring. It may tell us far more about the supervisor's prejudices, in fact, than it does about the paraprofessionals' ability. Mugnier, herself, surmises that the supervisors seeing little difference in performance were most likely members of the same group who elsewhere in the survey indicated that they didn't differentiate in assignments between librarians and library associates.[3] Once again we are reminded of the power of self-fulfilling prophecy.

St. Clair and Aluri take a different approach. They began by collecting a random sample of reference questions, categorizing them into four broad types—(1) directional, (2) instructional, (3) reference, and (4) extended reference—with several subdivisions in each. According to them, nonprofessionals with adequately planned training and an "orientation program" could have handled questions in the first two categories and part of the third.[4] They go on to point out that questions in these categories account for some 80%[5] of the questions asked, and inquire whether answering such questions is the best path for librarians "to achieve full faculty status".[6] They identify some of the shortcomings of their study by acknowledging the difficulty of assigning questions to appropriate categories and the failure to take into account user satisfaction and user-librarian communication. They fail, however, to reveal how they judged that questions in a given category could indeed be answered by a carefully trained "nonprofessional." Ironically, in an article intended to justify the use of paraprofessionals at the reference desk, the authors make unproven assumptions about the inabilities of non-M.L.S. staff.

Haldorsson and Murfin examine librarian-user communication in "The Performance of Professionals and Paraprofessionals in the Reference Interview." Using twenty-five sets of "indirect" and "faulty information" questions given to separate staffs, one made up of professionals and the other of paraprofessionals, the authors discovered significant differences between the two groups. Both performed adequately on indirect questions in which the patron asked for general information when he or she was actually seeking something more specific. Professionals performed appropriately 90% of the time in responding to patrons asking for a reference source when they really wanted information. Paraprofessionals responded appropriately only 50% of the time. Neither group did well in responding to questions containing faulty information, though the librarians' reactions should be termed adequate, though not "top quality."[7]

TRAINING, EDUCATION, AND STAFFING

Haldorsson and Murfin's conclusions deserve special attention. Along with their findings, findings that tell us more about how things are than about how they should be, the authors provide concrete suggestions about appropriate responses. On the one hand they suggest organizing the work load so that, contrary to the usual pattern, librarians would do all of the interviewing of patrons, referring easier questions to nonprofessionals. As an alternative they make several suggestions about training and education that would increase staff knowledge both in the communication process of the reference interview and in subject matter. To improve referral and consultation among staff they make several suggestions about changes in policy that should be implemented irrespective of staffing.

Of special note is the authors' repeated claim that their study tells us nothing about whether nonprofessionals "ought" to be used at the reference desk. They are correct insofar as they go, but their conclusions about the primacy of knowledge in reference service should influence supervisors making the necessarily pragmatic decisions of whom to hire and assign to the desk. Any question about reference service requiring a broad educational background along with training in the use of libraries and their resources would do well to consider Haldorsson and Murfin's documentation of the value of personal knowledge in dealing with "faulty information" questions. Their study leads them to call for "the selection of nonprofessional personnel . . . both on the basis of high education level and library science courses."

Similarly, Mason and Mason's recent article, "The Whole Shebang—Comprehensive Evaluation of Reference Operations," calls for paraprofessionals with "educational and intellectual attainments nearly at the level of professionals, plus walloping amounts of training in all aspects of reference work continually."[8] Both articles prescribe an objective that could be beyond the ability of the local labor market to supply, and supervisors need to consider that fact in determining staffing.

The two articles also make prescriptions that could exceed the capacity of the local library. Haldorsson and Murfin's call for in-service education aimed at increasing subject knowledge presupposes staff and money to provide such experience. Both resources (as with so many others in libraries) are in short supply. Staff need time to organize or prepare in-service education. They also need time to attend the in-service sessions (which invariably snarl already complicated desk schedules). Still more they need the expertise in conducting sessions that makes the training effective. In-service training provided by non-staff members usually costs money as well as time. If the library is unwilling or unable to pay, this effectively limits even those staff members willing to attend outside regular work hours.

Boyer and Theimer's research in the use and training of paraprofessionals in academic libraries—where one might expect higher educational levels—found that 40% lacked the baccalaureate degree. Even more disheartening was their discovery that 80% of the libraries surveyed provided no formal in-service training.[9]

Mason and Mason argue that it "takes ten years of avid reading in a broad range of fields after a good liberal education" just to provide the perspective necessary for even the first step in answering a reference query.[10] They may overstate their case slightly, but the implication is accurate that in-service education by itself is insufficient. Reference staff must bring a substantial amount on their own to their jobs. Libraries cannot, and apparently do not, make up for the inadequacy of their local pool of candidates for a job.

PERSONNEL POLICIES, SALARIES, AND EQUITY

Another factor related to personnel availability affects staffing patterns. Many libraries operate under some type of employee classification scheme that effectively limits their options when filling a position. Care must be taken when devising or revising such schemes to provide the flexibility that allows the library to hire the best available person. Differences between levels of reference workers should allow for promotion on the basis of expertise and performance. Employees with specialized knowledge deserve recognition for their unique qualities. However, such a policy should not penalize generalists whose strength lies in the breadth of their background. Their special talents enable them to know a little bit about everything and then bring that knowledge to bear on a seemingly obscure request. Library staff deserve alternatives to administrative positions as a means of promotion. Otherwise we condemn our patrons to help either from neophytes or from frustrated, dead-ended employees.

Discussions of the use of professionals and nonprofessionals at the reference desk rarely mention salary other than by saying how using paraprofessionals will save money for the library. Equally interesting is how librarians discussing comparable *worth* rarely mention the nonprofessional at the reference desk who may be doing comparable *work*. Though I know of one library that based its decision to stop using paraprofessionals at the desk partly out of concern for the potential of a grievance or lawsuit based on equal pay for equal work, I believe it was exceptional in its concern.

Fortunately one of its other concerns was the larger moral issue of equity and fairness. Paraprofessionals I have spoken with over the past eight years have all been sensitive about their treatment by "professional" librarians who, the paraprofessionals imply or state openly, possess varying amounts of arrogance. Compounding their resentment is their perception of the inequity of salaries. A library that cannot justify its salary differences should think carefully about its use of paraprofessionals and its wage scales. Blatant hypocrisy ill becomes any institution, but in libraries, where salaries are always small, the hypocrisy seems to come cheap.

Of greater import than hypocrisy is the impact inequity has on morale. Though not mentioned by name, morale is certainly one of the factors Lancaster includes in his recent discussion of why studies show that the probability of complete success in obtaining reference answers is so low.[11]

CONCLUSION

No single answer exists to the question of whether one should use paraprofessionals at the reference desk. Quality of service remains the bottom line in making the decision, but until we develop the tools for evaluating the quality of both the service and the personnel, we will continue to find it hard to justify our choices. That the choices we make sometimes seem self-serving should spur us on in the effort. Meanwhile, decisions have to be made, and supervisors should look carefully at such issues as local personnel and personnel policies, training resources, and equity to avoid short-sighted focus on just one part of their budgets. As with all important issues, simple answers do not exist.

REFERENCES

1. Charlotte Mugnier, *The Paraprofessional and the Professional Job Structure*, Chicago: American Library Association, 1980, p. 41.
2. Jeffrey W. St. Clair and Rao Aluri, "Staffing the Reference Desk: Professionals or Nonprofessionals," *Journal of Academic Librarianship* 3(July 1977): 149-153.
3. Mugnier, p. 57.
4. St. Clair and Aluri, p. 152.
5. Another interesting example of the eighty-twenty rule. A delightful coincidence here is that if one assumed (however inaccurately) that paraprofessionals possessed the baccalaureate degree, but not the M.L.S., they would have eighty per cent of a "professional" education. How appropriate then that they can answer eighty per cent of the questions. Though not a cause-effect relationship, it's a wonderful correlation.
6. St. Clair and Aluri, p. 152.
7. Egill A. Haldorsson and Marjorie E. Murfin, "The Performance of Professionals and Nonprofessionals in the Reference Interview," *College and Research Libraries* 38(September 1977): 385-395.
8. Ellsworth Mason and Joan Mason, "The Whole Shebang—Comprehensive Evaluation of Reference Operations," *The Reference Librarian* 11(Fall/Winter 1984): 36.
9. Laura M. Boyer and William C. Theimer, Jr., "The Use and Training of Nonprofessional Personnel at Reference Desks in Selected College and University Libraries," *College and Research Libraries* 36(May 1975):197.
10. Mason and Mason, p. 38.
11. F.W. Lancaster, "Factors Influencing the Effectiveness of Question-Answering Services in Libraries," *The Reference Librarian* 11(Fall/Winter 1984):105.

End-User Searching:
The Beginning or the End?

Geraldene Walker

The availability of machine-readable indexes (databases) for online searching from remote locations has expanded the scope of traditional reference service in libraries. The number of reference sources available in this form has increased exponentially during the last decade, and more and more libraries of all types now offer an online search service as an additional source of information. The role of the librarian as the intermediary between the user and his information requirement has extended the search skills needed and enhanced the reputation of the information professional. Until recently most users have not been prepared to invest the time and effort required to learn these skills themselves, and have been happy to permit the information specialist to interpret their requests and to search for information on their behalf. In this situation the user's role has been the elaboration of the query, the provision of subject expertise and the evaluation of the retrieved document sets to provide feedback on relevance.

The recent spread of personal microcomputers which can be used as remote access terminals containing both memory and intelligence, has altered this situation. These search services, originally designed for use by trained personnel, are now freely available to end-users with little or no searching training or experience. The era of direct end-user access to these online services has begun. A combination of lower prices and simplified access protocols has led to increased numbers of end-users performing their own searches on these systems.

The author is a former member of the faculty of the College of Librarianship, Wales. She is currently enrolled in the doctoral program at School of Information Studies at Syracuse University, Syracuse, NY 13210.

NEW INFORMATION SOURCES

The first tangible sign of this change manifested itself about six years ago when the idea of making use of cheap night-time capacity on mainframes, telephone lines and data communication networks for the transmission of data to microcomputers during non-business hours was proposed in *Business Week*. Electronic publishing was still in its infancy, but many publishers were interested in the possibility of making their full-text files available online, and the commercial market appeared ready for such developments. (Almost everything which now appears online is supplied by publishers, and most of it it also available in other forms such as print, radio or television.)

The first such service, The Source, was introduced as an "information utility" in June 1979, and quickly enrolled a core of subscribers. It has been followed by a number of other such information sources aimed at the end-user market—Compuserve, Delphi, Dow Jones News/Retrieval, Nexis and Newsnet. Most of these organizations in fact provide a variety of services beyond information retrieval, including up-to-date news and stock quotations, financial analysis, electronic mail, electronic shopping, games, travel services and electronic conferencing.

Although these new systems have been designed specifically for end-users, their use has not yet expanded at the expected rate, mainly because they are overly complex—especially when one realizes that they are in direct competition with such habitual behavior patterns as a simple phonecall to a travel agent or a mail-order store. It would seem that the mere availability of a service, however convenient and advantageous, does not necessarily produce a market for that service. In fact, the reverse is probably true—the need must be present before a suitable service is acceptable. Nevertheless, it seems reasonable to assume that these electronic services will be more widely adopted in the near future as increased numbers of people purchase their own personal microcomputers and become interested in other online sources of information.

SYSTEM ADAPTATIONS

The traditional providers of online information services at an organizational level, the major vendors, have not been slow to recognize the possibilities for expansion provided by this new end-user market. But they have also realized the need to adapt their present systems, designed for use by trained professional searchers, to meet the needs of naive users working unsupervised and unassisted in their own homes and offices. A number of these vendors are now marketing alternative, simplified versions of their standard systems for use during non-business hours. Examples include DIALOG's Knowledge Index, BRS/After Dark, Sci-mate from ISI and SDC's Searchmaster.

These simplified systems are designed to assist with the various areas of expertise required for online searching. Girard and Moreau[1] have identified three different levels of competence:

1. Knowledge of the database being searched, its coverage, its indexing philosophy, the type of vocabulary control and how it is applied, and the bibliographic elements contained in the records.
2. Knowledge of the search system, its retrieval program, the command language and how the database is loaded.
3. Knowledge of the subject involved in the search, the development of its concepts, together with the vocabulary and structure associated with it in the language of the database.

The proliferation of available systems requires that the searcher not only acquire a variety of command languages, but also learn a full range of search options, and be constantly aware of current enhancements, which is especially difficult for occasional users. Certain aspects of database knowledge (with hundreds of databases now available), particularly features such as currency and indexing policy, are completely foreign to most untrained users, whose approach will tend towards a simple natural language search. Most intermediaries tend to specialize in a group of databases within a particular subject field, and research has repeatedly shown that all searchers have a preferred file which they tend to access first, regardless of its apparent suitability.[2] The adapted systems offer a reduced number of these databases, with menu-based selection to simplify the choice of file. Unfortunately, the CROS file of BRS and DIALINDEX on DIALOG, which provide users with posting figures for particular subject terms in different databases, are not available on BRS/After Dark and Knowledge Index. Nichol[3] argues reasonably that this proliferation of databases increases the need for assistance in the search process from a trained intermediary.

Knowledge of the subject area to be searched is the one area where the user is accepted as the expert, though many intermediaries do have advanced degress within the subject areas which they normally search. The major advantage for end-user searching is the elimination of the reference interview, a recognized source of "noise" within the search process. The user is no longer required to attempt to translate his information need for understanding by a third party, and this appears to be a major advantage. On the other hand, the preliminary discussion involved in the reference interview may possibly clarify the nature of his information need to the user, as well as informing the intermediary.

Knowledge Index is the DIALOG version of this type of user-friendly frontend. It provides an interface between the information-seeker and a subset of the DIALOG databases during restricted hours (evenings and weekends). Access is to twenty-six databases grouped into fourteen sections (as of Fall 1984), via a subset of the command language. The intention is to retain the full power and flexibility of the DIALOG software, while at the same time making it easy for use by novice searchers. In fact, the simplification is mainly a change in command vocabulary, with some restrictions on system facilities. One helpful feature is the availability of online "help" commands, especially in view of the typical user's desire to try the system before consulting the manual! The documents for the retrieved citations may also be ordered while online, though this service is relatively expensive. The workbook for Knowledge Index provides a "crash course" in both the theory and mechanics of searching, with many useful examples. For a more detailed evaluation of Knowledge Index and the features it offers see Ojala.[4]

The BRS version of this type of system, known as After Dark, is advertised as an information resource for "business people, educators, attorneys, physicians, writers and students, in fact, anyone with a need for up-to-date comprehensive summaries of the most recent information in virtually any field." This service again offers access to a subset of the regular databases (thirty-five as of March 1984) during evening hours (6pm to midnight) and at weekends, for a fraction of the daytime cost ($6 to $20). Although a user manual comes with the subscription to this service, the system is really designed to be learned interactively online. It is menu-based, with two tracks (modes of operation) available—one for beginners and one for experienced searchers (the "fast-track"). In fact, some of the more sophisticated features of the full BRS system (such as truncation, stacking and variable print formats) are also now available on After Dark. Thus, using the "fast-track" is not very different from using the full BRS system, but with a slightly different command language designed to be easier to use (though experienced searchers are reported to find it rather difficult to adapt to its user-friendly protocols). For a detailed analysis of system features see Dolan.[5]

SOFTWARE PACKAGES

An alternative mode of assistance for users' information gathering is the use of communications software, designed to provide connections from micros to remote mainframes for access to and transfer of files. Recently, some online vendors have been marketing "dedicated" communications packages to simplify access to their services, but many other packages are also available commercially. These software offerings vary enormously in complexity, from simple assistance with communications protocols and downloading of files (Perfect Link and Crosstalk), to searching assistance with searching a single database (Sourcelink and the Market Analyser), a group of data bases (Searchhelper), a complete online system (Insearch and Searchmaster), or even with accessing a range of systems (PFS Access and SuperScout). This "gateway" or access software makes searching easier in several ways. Firstly, it automatically handles the communication and log-on protocols by allowing the user to customise his "profile" to disk. The search itself is simplified by the provision of menus for selection at each stage of the search process—particularly helpful with difficult areas such as database selection, search term combination and strategy alteration while online. This type of software also saves on connect-time costs, since search strategies can be prepared offline and uploaded, and retrieved references can be downloaded for later scanning and evaluation offline. The big advantage of these "dedicated" packages is their ease of use. For further details on communications software see Holland[6] and for a comparison of a number of gateway packages see Levy.[7]

END-USER SEARCHING

In view of these moves aimed at the encouragement of end-user searching, information regarding the search performance of such users is of interest. A number of studies have been reported on the effectiveness and feasibility of searching on the full systems in operational scientific and technical settings. Richardson[8] focused on scientists and engineers at the Raytheon Company's Submarine Signal Division, and discovered that, while all participants were able to use the system successfully, levels of usage were astonishingly low, particularly bearing in mind that searches during the first seven months of the project were free. Richardson concluded from this that the mere availability of a new search service does not necessarily change the information-gathering patterns of users. On the other hand, a study by Haines[9] in a similar high technology environment (Eastman-Kodak Research Laboratories) found that users of very specific and highly organized databases (such as the various chemical search files) preferred to do their own searches, rather than try to explain their information need to an intermediary.

Walton and Dedert,[10] reporting on system use by a small number of end-users at Exxon Research and Engineering Company, comment on the difficulty of the search process for casual and infrequent users. High initial enthusiasm evaporated in the face of the time and effort necessary to master and retain search skills. These authors suggest that end-users should only be encouraged to perform routine searches using author or natural language search keys, and that intermediary assistance should be retained for comprehensive search problems—at "least until such time as the entire search process can be done automatically."

The recent availability of database access software and the easy-to-use evening online services from the major vendors discussed earlier are a move towards automating searching for the non-specialist market. These hardware and software developments have broadened the end-user environment, and recently a small number of studies have been published which report on naive searching in general academic settings using software enhancements and user-friendly interfaces. Although most of the literature on this topic is descriptive in nature—what is available and how it works—two studies of end-users have reported on the use of BRS/After Dark by untrained users in library settings.

Janke[11] reported on a pilot survey of end-user searching held in March 1983 at the University of Ottawa. The library computer search service was opened to end-user searching for twenty-five clients on an experimental basis, with the selection of searchers being based on the suitability of the user's request (databases available on After Dark, number of references required and acceptable turn-around time). In response to a questionnaire, users found the menu-driven protocols and commands easy to use, and felt "comfortable" with the hardware, despite little familiarity with computers or telecommunications. Some trained searchers have expressed doubt regarding the precision of this simplified searching, but Janke found that for over 50% of his users, over 60% of the items they retrieved were "highly relevant." Recall, on the other hand, must be questionable, even though it is probably true that most users generally have low recall requirements. 72% of Janke's users claimed that they would be willing to run all their own searches in the future, so long as technical help would be available if required (such as in cases of hardware or software malfunction). He concludes that the BRS interface overcomes the barrier to access for infrequent searchers, and he claims that, while the need for librarian search analysts will remain for some years in order to perform complex searches requiring involved search strategies or multi-database access, in the longterm all end-users will perform their own searches using their personal microcomputers.

In a followup study the same author[12] notes the rapid spread of end-user searching in over thirty academic libraries in Canada and the United States, and attributes it to aggressive marketing, growing awareness of the available systems and the increasing ease of use. At the University of Ottawa during the past year almost 15% of all online searches were performed by users themselves. Despite the success of such searching, Janke concludes that "the operation of an effective end-user search service depends a great deal on the provision of professional supportive services" [p18].

A similar study at the University of Wisconsin-Stout is reported by Trzebiatowski[13] where twenty searches by students and faculty were conducted using BRS/After Dark. (Both Knowledge Index and After Dark were considered for the study, with BRS being selected as more user-friendly, less expensive and covering a larger number of databases). Users were given a pre-search orientation session, covering both the system and the hardware. 60% found the search easier than expected, and 85% considered the results were "good" or "excellent." It appeared that strategy formulation was the most difficult aspect of searching, though this might have been due to overconfidence, since some commands (notably truncation) were used incorrectly. On the other hand, personal experience with student users at Syracuse University using the Insearch package suggests that database selection was their biggest problem. All researchers find novice users much slower than intermediaries—the Madison study quotes 26.98 minutes average per end-user search, as compared with 7.1 minutes for the intermediaries. This suggests that much of the user's connect time is "wasted" by lack of proper preparation. Trzebiatowski concludes that infrequent end-users will need considerable instruction in certain aspects of searching—choosing an appropriate database, selecting alternative search terms and constructing a search strategy. It is worth noting that both these studies emphasize the need, at least in the short-term, for trained professional searchers.

LIBRARY ALTERNATIVES

It has already been shown that the spread of microcomputers and the development of user-friendly software enhancements are making a wide variety of online retrieval systems increasingly available to untrained users. So far libraries have provided the principal market for the online service vendors, but this picture is obviously changing as access becomes easier. It is clear that online searching will become even easier in the future, and will probably become a general professional skill acquired by all. This is already happening on a small scale—business managers and consultants in particular are currently accessing online sources for their work-related information needs using their own personal computers. But current online use is only a small part of the potential market. Eventually all libraries will have to open their online search services to personal searching or lose the confidence of their users. The role of the library and the longterm survival of the online intermediary are being seriously questioned in the professional literature. A selection of titles such as "Change or be Changed"[14] "Managing Revolutions"[15] and "Adaption, Extinction or Genetic Drift"[16] speak for themselves. All writers emphasize the need for change at an organizational level and for viewing information provision in its broadest sense. It will be necessary for libraries to adapt and expand their services and for the roles of library personnel to change.

Some users may still wish to have their queries searched online by library staff, in the same way that some users prefer to ask for assistance from reference staff in the manual situation. Some requests on databases not available via the user-friendly systems will obviously require the assistance of a trained intermediary, and some searches will be too complicated for the end-user to manage on his own. Thus, it seems likely that the solution of the more sophisticated problems will still fall to the intermediary. So far it is not known how large a proportion of users will wish to perform their online searches for themselves. Janke recently found about 14.8% of users in an academic library environment were so inclined—nearly double the 7.3% found by Wanger et al.[17] only eight years earlier. It seems reasonable to predict that this rate of increase is likely to continue, though some searching will still remain to be done by the intermediary.

One may have reservations regarding the performance of these "do-it-yourself" searchers, despite the fact that they appear to be reasonably satisfied with their own performance in terms of the relevance of what they retrieve. End-user searching has been compared with that of trained searchers using the original systems. Fenichel[18] compared searchers with different levels of experience using the full systems and found that the experienced searchers generally achieved better recall, though this is not necessarily a desirable feature, since large numbers of users are only interested in finding a few "good" references. She also found that more experienced searchers searched faster and therefore performed "cheaper" searches, since they spent less time online. Online cost-effectiveness figures have traditionally ignored the cost of staff time, and are thus unfairly weighted against end-users in direct comparisons. In the future user performance can obviously be expected to improve with the use of a user-friendly interface.

In any case, it seems likely that performance figures are somewhat superfluous—the move towards self-searching would be impossible to halt. Both Janke and Trzebiatowski reported that most of their users who performed their own searches enjoyed the experience, were satisfied with their results, and were eager to repeat the experience. Similar reactions were obtained from a small group of undergraduate students who searched DIALOG using two of the menu-based systems at Syracuse University.[19] They proved to be enthusiastic and competent—and eager to use such systems again in the future. Halperin and Pagell[20] also report that students at the Wharton School of the University of Pennsylvania "strongly agreed" with statements concerning the usefulness of online search systems and their ease of use, and stated that they were satisfied that they retrieved useful material.

One future role for the intermediary will be as trainer and advisor to those users who wish to perform their own searches. Halperin emphasizes the commitment of staff time necessary to monitor an end-user search service, particularly when it is offered free of charge and is thus likely to be heavily used. His service had staff responsible for logging on all searchers, organizing a system of booking and providing instruction sheets, as well as helping with the actual search itself. The most notable changes he remarked were a sharp decline in intermediary searching, and an increase in pressure on library resources as more materials were brought to the attention of users via citations retrieved online. Any library offering such a service will need to provide systems backup and liaison for hardware and software, as well as system documentation. Training courses must be arranged for groups of end-users, with library staff in the role of instructors. Intermediaries also need to be present while searchers are at the keyboard, at least for a time, so as to assist in cases of difficulty. Experience indicates that most end-users feel more confident with the knowledge that help is at hand if it should be required.

One area still remains in which the role of the library is unchallenged—document provision. The spread of online bibliographic search systems and end-use searching is making users aware of enormous amounts of information beyond that which is available locally. In general, such materials can only be accessed through local libraries via inter-library loans procedures not normally available on an individual basis, or through the expensive online order systems. It is a well-known fact that any increase in online searching goes hand-in-hand with an increase in inter-library loan requests. Librarians can assist this provision and can advise on what materials are available locally, and how to obtain those which are not. Some parts of the retrieved citations are often in abbreviated form, and users may well also require assistance in intepreting their output. Librarians can provide a variety of these "value-added" services to users who wish to perform their own searches, and it is also important that those searches still performed by the intermediary shall be seen as customized, quality products—screened, sorted and if possible evaluated and annotated.

Today's so-called 'information society' has revolutionized the availability of information and our modes of access to it. Computers and telecommunications networks are part of our everyday life. The information professional is at the heart of these developments, which have so far remained largely unorganized at a national level. We have the choice between attempting to retain our positions in control of the means of access to information, or of expanding those roles to include the training of others in self-help.

OTHER OPPORTUNITIES

These suggestions, while accepting the reality of and necessity for change, still assume the idea of information provisions as a conventional, institutionalized service. But some staff may feel that their roles have been diminished by technological developments within libraries, and may wish to look further afield. As moves towards distributed data processing, electronic publishing and communication, and end-user database searching gather momentum, the qualified information professional will find increasing opportunities outside the traditional information-providing institutions.

A new role is emerging within corporate and administrative contexts for information resource managers. The librarian's knowledge of fields such as communications technology and data processing, and our professional organizing and information-gathering skills make us ideally qualified for such employment. These same talents, together with subject analysis skills such as cataloging, indexing and abstracting, will also be appropriate for positions within the information-providing sector. As more information becomes available in machine-readable form and is available through the online service vendors, increased numbers of qualified professional staff will be required for subject indexing, for database design and for organizing and mounting computer files.

Outside the institutional setting altogether, professional skills are also in demand on the open market. Small numbers of information professionals are already marketing their skills as consultants on a part-time basis. This sideline can be developed into a full-time occupation, particularly if combined with the provision of instructional courses.

Information as a commodity to be capitalized and costed is the attitude of this sector of the information industry. One way of making use of reference and online search skills in the open market is the job of the information broker, who acts as an interface between a client and an information source, and charges for that service. Cost plus a pre-determined profit margin is the usual pricing strategy, and effectiveness is measured by the levels of repeat business and referrals. There is a fine line between the consultant and the information specialist, with the first providing information and analysis, and the second information-gathering skills. Both fall within our areas of expertise. This free-lance field has also recruited from a variety of professions in the past, so competition is fierce, but the majority are still trained librarians.

These fee-based information services vary enormously in size and volume of business. They are almost all located near large metropolitan areas, and the smaller services rely largely on local business within a restricted geographical area. Many of them are one-man (or woman) oganizations. Originally the role of this type of information specialist was mainly to act as the intermediary who provided access to online databases. With the current increasing end-user involvement in that area, the specialist's role is expanding to provide evaluative, analytical and packaging services for all types of information. The specialist activities involved in addition to online searching vary—the preparation of bibliographies, document delivery, SDI, consultancy and general research—often supplemented with publishing, indexing and training activities.

It is worth noting that this segment of the information industry is particularly vulnerable to technological developments and the expanding knowledge and sophistication of clients. As a wider range of information is becoming available to end-users from a range of sources, there is an increasing move by professionals towards validation, interpretation and evaluation services. The concept of information as a commodity is becoming widely accepted in our information-dependent society, and people are becoming more willing to pay for it. These new opportunities require an expanded outlook and entrepreneurial skills, often foreign to the traditional professional scene. An emphais on technology, inter-personal skills and contacts, marketing, and management will be the decisive factors. The skills that a person with library or information science training possesses are certainly relevant in the broad information environment, but horizons will need to be expanded and new skills learned and developed. Most of all, the challenge is to market our skills.

REFERENCES

1. Anne Girard and Magdeleine Moreau: "An examination of the role of the intermediary in the online searching of chemical literature." *Online Review* 5(3), June 1981, p.217-225.

2. Raya Fidel: "Online searching styles: a case-study-based model of searching behavior." *Journal of the American Society for Information Science* 35(4), July 1984, p.211-221.
3. Kathleen M. Nichol: "Data base proliferation implications for librarians." *Special Libraries* 74(4), April 1983, p.110-118.
4. Marydee Ojala: "Knowledge Index: a review." *Online* 7(5), September 1983, p.31-33.
5. Donna R. Dolan: "Offlines: databases for everyman." *Database* 6(4), December 1983, p.101-104.
6. Maurita Peterson Holland: "Communications software: experiences with Perfect Link and Crosstalk XVI." *Online* 8(4) July 1984, p.75-80.
7. Louise R. Levy: "Gateway software: is it for you?" *Online* 8(6), November 1984, p.67-79.
8. Robert J. Richardson: "End-user online searching in a high-technology engineering environment." *Online* 5(4), October 1981, p.44-57.
9. Judith S. Haines: "Experiences in training end-user searchers." *Online* 6(6), November 1982, p.14-23.
10. Kenneth R. Walton and Patricia L. Dedert: "Experiences at Exxon in training end-users to search technical databases online." *Online* 7(5), September 1983, p.42-50.
11. Richard V. Janke: "BRS/After Dark: the birth of online self-service." *Online* 7(5), September 1983, p.12-29.
12. Richard V. Janke: "Online after six: end user searching comes of age." *Online* 8(6), November 1984, p.15-29.
13. Elaine Trzebiatowski: "End user study on BRS/After Dark." *RQ* 23(4), Summer 1984, p.446- 450.
14. Dennis A. Lewis: "Today's challenge—tomorrow's choice: change or be changed or the Doomsday Scenario Mk.2." *Journal of Information Science* 2(2), 1980, p.59-74.
15. Patricia W. Berger: "Managing revolutions: coping with evolving information technologies." *Special Libraries* 71(9), September 1980, p.386-397.
16. Blaise Cronin: "Adaption, extinction or genetic drift." *Aslib Proceedings* 35(6/7), June/July 1983, p.278-289.
17. Judith Wanger, D. McDonald and M. C. Berger: *Evaluation of the online search process: a final report.* Santa Monica, CA.: Cuadra Associates, 1980 (PB81-132565).
18. Carol Fenichel: "Online searching: measures which discriminate among users with different types of experiences." *Journal of the American Society for Information Science* 32(1), January 1981, p.23-32.
19. Geraldene Walker and Michael Eisenberg: "Assisting the end-user: an analysis of alternative approaches." Paper presented at the 14th ASIS Mid-Year Meeting, Fort Lauderdale, Florida, May 20-22, 1985.
20. Michael Halperin and Ruth A. Pagell: "Free 'do-it-yourself' online searching . . . what to expect." *Online* 9(2), March 1985, p.82-84.

Staff Sharing: A Development Program

Joan W. Jensen

For almost ten years an effective program for staff development has been in place at the University of Connecticut's Homer Babbidge Library, providing library staff with opportunities to develop new skills and a broader understanding of library operations. Staff sharing provides a structure which allows any staff member to work in a defined role in another department for a few hours each week. The overall program is made up of a group of as many as eight departmental offerings. Control of each program rests with the departments, including responsibility for definition, training, and evaluation. For them, the primary benefit is the practical one of gaining assistance to meet daily needs. For the library administration the benefits which make this program popular are that it operates within the existing structure using staff skills at the department level to plan and operate each program. The participants gain knowledge and satisfaction, and they are at the same time making a direct contribution to the operation of the library.

Structure

The strength of the program is derived from two opposing elements. Basic administrative guidelines, written in 1975, remain valid and in place, and as long as the guidelines are adhered to, many component programs can operate with as much flexibility as each sponsoring department desires. The guidelines require that a program description be submitted, approved, and reviewed annually. The prospectus for a staff sharing activity will include a description, definition of limits (such as number of participants, number of years on the program), criteria for selection, an outline of the train-

---

Ms. Jensen is Head, Reference Department, The University of Connecticut, Storrs, CT 06268.

ing proposed, and the system of evaluation to be used. Staff participation is limited to no more than three hours a week. These modest limits were originally set to reassure supervisors, hard pressed to meet daily needs, that the drain on staff time would not be intolerable. The limits have proved acceptable and may well be a key factor in the successful expansion of the program into many departments. Applications are accepted only once a year, and coincide with the evaluation of participants and existing programs. This formality provides excellent control—for example, an ineffective program can be terminated, or a staff member rejected for a program of choice can be given a clear explanation. Evaluation, although it takes time and can be burdensome in the early stages, encourages adaptation of programs to increase their effectiveness. It is expected to be a two-way process; participants are asked to evaluate their experience on a program. When a staff sharing activity has been improved to a point where it is consistently successful, the administrative burden tends to lessen in direct proportion to the benefits derived.

Scope

Creating reasonable desk schedules which will allow staff adequate, uninterrupted time to complete their other responsibilities is a constant need for public service departments. Not surprisingly, the first staff sharing programs addressed this, offering opportunities to work at service desks. These have been popular with staff from technical service departments who enjoy having an opportunity to work directly with the public, and also gain perspective by seeing the end product of their behind-scenes labors. Because this library has many service points, several staff sharing programs requiring differing levels of skill have become available. They include basic instruction to users of the card catalog, or provide direction in locating serials, as well as supplementary assistance to librarians at reference, government publications, maps, and special collections service desks. A surprise early in the program was the high interest among librarians in experiencing alternative roles. Early participants in the Reference Assistant Program included the music librarian, a cataloger, a special collections librarian, and an acquisitions librarian. They were seeking a broader understanding of another professional skill, and their active involvement made a substantial contribution toward improved interdepartmental relationships.

Even more encouraging has been the recent growth of programs being offered by technical departments and the willingness of public service personnel to work behind the scenes. Reluctance on the part of technical service departments to offer programs (due perhaps to the belief that a partially trained person might not be effective) has been overcome and opportunities now exist for staff to do pre-order searching on OCLC, file in the public catalog, catalog manuscripts and archives, or check in serials. Offering a practical method through which to improve understanding of each other's roles, staff sharing can bridge the gap which still tends to separate technical and public service departments. Even more important, it offers diversification for those who might have become stale in a specific assignment. Such a program is one of the possibilities for coping with staffing difficulties suggested by William Miller in his perceptive article "What's Wrong With Reference?"[1]

The variety of offerings and the general acceptance of staff sharing as it has developed over the years has meant that it attracts staff from all departments and from all levels. Participants range from those whose normal activities include checkpoint control to the Library Director. In selecting participants, those who run staff sharing activities are encouraged to think in terms of the applicant's abilities as they relate to the work to be done, not necessarily on formal educational background. Experience on the job may be a key factor. Criteria may need to be established for certain programs, but a promising candidate who offers a special background will be considered.

THE REFERENCE ASSISTANT PROGRAM

This was the first staff sharing endeavor, a prototype the success of which later encouraged development of other staff sharing activities. The Reference Assistant Program is no longer evaluated in terms of whether or not it is successful—its place in the department's service structure has long been fully accepted. Initially, however, introducing a program that would use nonprofessionals at the reference desk in a conservative reference department was controversial. The first steps were tentative, and acceptance among the established reference staff was by no means immediate. A recent article by Courtois and Goetsch addresses this issue of using nonprofessionals at reference desks.[2] They summarize pertinent literature, and provide an analysis of their research which involved gathering detailed information from more than sixty four-year academic institutions. The experience of the Homer Babbidge Library's reference department closely parallels their findings: nonprofessionals can be used effectively and become an integral part of reference service; training must be given special attention; interaction between professional and nonprofessional in the service environment to ensure proper referral is of the utmost importance; and enhancement of the roles of both professional and nonprofessional staff is likely to result.

Encouragement to begin the Reference Assistant Program came from outside the department. The library administration was feeling pressure for diversification, some form of staff development, from well qualified nonprofessional library staff. At the same time, reference librarians were heeding the message to enter the classroom to provide bibliographic instruction, which made them less available for desk coverage. In spite of the time needed for training assistants, it is doubtful that the flourishing instruction program now offered would have been possible without the nine-to-eighteen hours of desk assistance provided by the Reference Assistant Program each semester. The eventual expansion of the staff sharing concept library-wide more than met the administrative need for an economic way of providing a staff development opportunity.

Criteria

Because there was controversy, considerable care was taken by the personnel director and the head of reference to develop the initial program guidelines. As previously noted, not only have these proved lastingly effective, but they were also used to structure other staff sharing activities. They mirror procedures for hiring new staff. A program description, like a job description, defines limits and sets criteria. To aid in selection, the limits include the number of participants who can be accepted, and the requirement that an applicant must have taken a reference course. Detailed applications are submitted on standard forms, providing sufficient background information, together with authorization from the applicant's department head. Being able to share information about assistants' special experience and qualifications has been helpful in establishing mutual respect between them and the reference staff. Selection is made after the applicants have been interviewed by the person responsible for the program, who also evaluates them on a continuous basis as well as formally through a written statement at the end of the program year. As previously noted, professional staff assessed the guidelines, saw themselves as qualified, and applied to participate, thus tending to neutralize the professional/nonprofessional issue.

Training

If a staff sharing activity is to offer sufficient depth to meet staff development goals, training must be undertaken by someone sufficiently skilled who is willing to plan, instruct and reinforce as needed. Although training can be a shared responsibility in a departmental program, it requires coordination and a serious commitment of time. Recognition of this need can be a stumbling block, causing some to reject the staff sharing concept because it offers too little in return. Those who have been bold and persistent, however, sincerely believe that in the long run the effort invested in training can be worthwhile. The responsibility for running a departmental program is often delegated to a senior staff member who may be interested in developing administrative skills.

The Reference Assistant Program provides a continuing opportunity to consider what training is needed for reference work at the desk, and what is effective.[3] It should be noted that Reference Assistants are desk assistants, but that on this program they always work in tandem with an experienced reference librarian. Because of time constraints felt by both reference librarians and assistants, training ideas are not always followed up as well as they might be, nor can sufficient discussions be held, but a great deal has been learned.

Early evaluation showed that the original training plan was not working well. Assistants reported that they retained little of the detailed information on subject sources which was being provided by means of preliminary lectures, and that actual desk experience was far more useful. Present practice provides a general overview (orientation, procedures, expectations) followed by regular assignment at the desk to observe and then participate as appropriate. Over a period of two semesters, depth is added by attendance at reference seminars. These are conducted by librarians according to their subject specialty. The organized review of sources required also provides the reference librarians an excellent opportunity to refresh their own knowledge.

This program has not provided answers to the questions which Effie Astbury raised in 1973: "Has an effective system for screening questions as patrons present them at the reference desk yet been devised?'' and "How can a supervisor effectively exercise surveillance over an assistant's contacts with the patrons?''[4] In fact, little attempt is made to screen or sort questions, but this has not been a major problem. Reference assistants are expected to recognize when there is need for referral. The importance of proper analysis of the question and recognizing the hidden need is emphasized during training. Reference librarians are encouraged to work cooperatively with assistants, continuing the training process during actual reference work. Because this is a staff development program, participants have tended to be highly motivated, regarding their participation as a learning experience which never ends, and so are willing to seek advice when finding themselves in difficulty.[5] They are comfortable with the title and role of assistant, accepting the limits of what can be accomplished in so few hours a week. Those who are able to stay with the program for several years become valued members of the reference desk team.

Working with a variety of assistants has been beneficial to established reference staff. The infusion of different personalities has produced a heightened awareness of the importance of good interpersonal skills, providing opportunities to observe what is and what is not effective in working with the public, regardless of depth of specific knowledge of sources. Some assistants have demonstrated a natural ability in the public service role and have been encouarged to pursue their library studies with reference librarianship as a goal. Paradoxically, as the Reference Assistant Program frees reference librarians to pursue other activities, it also requires that, in training others, they pay regular, organized attention to the basics of good reference service. Charles A. Bunge in his article "Potential and reality at the reference desk: reflections on a return to the field" suggests that it is important for reference librarians to keep a good perspective on their professional skills if they are to retain joy in their profession. Some librarians find that working with new, eager reference assistants provides just such an opportunity because they can share their reference knowledge in a more systematic way than is possible during normal reference desk activity.[6]

STAFF SHARING IN PERSPECTIVE

If popularity can be taken as a measure of success, the Homer Babbidge Library's Staff Sharing Program is successful, for at last count more than one-third of the staff was actively participating in seven different departments. But the concerns of those who are less enthusiastic are valid. Responses to them can point to long-term gains—that the training time invested does eventually reap more benefits than losses, or that the small number of hours spent on a program does eventually accrue to a solid contribution as the participant gains experience. However, it is true that the depth of the contribution rarely approaches that of staff who perform the activity as part of their normal work. Improvement of staff morale can be sensed, but not necessarily proven.

It is essential to recognize this program for what it is and not regard it either as an answer to understaffing or as a total program for staff development. If basic staffing is inadequate, no amount of staff sharing activity will, in the long run, prevent stress. Overextended, the high enthusiasm and commitment of staff is likely to fade. The potential for chaos in reference departments, for example, as staff add more and more activities is all too accurately assessed in the Miller article previously noted.[1] The limits of the present program may well have been reached. A department that is too sparsely staffed may be forced to give staff sharing a low priority whatever the longterm benefits.

Conclusion

This library's staff sharing idea works, the program is sound and lively, but it ought to be but one element in a rounded staff development plan. To use fully the existing knowledge and skills of staff is excellent, but their willingness to participate should not be exploited. In a 1978 article Martell and Dougherty discuss the importance of human resource development within an organization.[7] They also describe a rounded program of staff development at the University of California, Berkeley, General Library which required appointment of a full-time coordinator and a substantial commitment of funds ($110,000 or 1.7% of the library's annual operating budget). This kind of informed, planned involvement on the part of management is needed so that staff will be provided with a variety of developmental opportunities and will be exposed to the ideas of others from outside the known environment. A complete program would include visiting lecturers, professionally conducted workshops, and encouraging staff to participate in appropriate activities at other locations. Provision for continuing education, with financial support, is also a recognized goal for a library which has accepted the wisdom of encouraging staff to develop to their full potential.

REFERENCES

1. Miller, William. "What's wrong with reference: coping with success and failure at the reference desk." *American Libraries* 15, (May 1984): 303-306, 321-322.
2. Courtois, Martin P. and Goetsch, Lori A. "Use of nonprofessionals at reference desks." *College & Research Libraries* 45, 1984, p. 385-391.
3. Rothstein, Samuel. "The making of a reference librarian." *Library Trends* 31, (Winter, 1983): 375-399.

Rothstein in this survey of education for reference librarianship notes that "The overwhelming preponderance of reference education, as it is actually *acquired* by North American librarians, goes on outside the accredited library schools and very little indeed has been written about it. The real reference education seldom gets to stand up." The repetitive training experience being gained in this program could assist us in defining what is needed, and what works well in continuing education for reference librarianship.

4. Astbury, Effie C. "Library technicians and the reference service." *Canadian Library Journal* 26, (January 1969): 54-57.
5. Halldorsson, Egill A. and Murfin, Marjorie E. "The performance of professionals and nonprofessionals in the reference interview." *College & Research LIbraries* 36 (September 1977): 193-200.

Note suggestions for improving service when using nonprofessional staff, found to be accurate in experience gained at the Homer Babbidge Library.

6. Bunge, Charles A. "Potential and reality at the reference desk: reflections on a 'Return to the field'" *Journal of Academic Librarianship* 10, 1984, p. 128-133.
7. Martell, Charles and Dougherty, Richard M. "The role of continuing education and training in human resource development: an administrator's viewpoint." *Journal of Academic Librarianship* 4, 1978, p. 151-155.

The Reference Librarian in the Small Information Center: Selection and Training

Miriam H. Tees

The information center, or special library in its narrow sense, exists, as its name implies to provide information to the organization of which it is a part, in furtherance of the goals of the organization. It is not designed to be an educational resource or a cultural center, nor does it normally attempt to fulfill an archival or preservation function for its organization. Those working in it are employed to gather, organize, and provide information in an accurate and timely manner to other employees of the organization who will use this information in their own work for the organization.

The distinguishing feature of the special librarian is the strong service aspect of his or her work. The selection, acquisition, and organization of information exist entirely to support the function of providing information. Special librarians answer requests for information but also become aware of the interests of users so that these users may be kept informed of current and new developments of use to them in their work.

Though there are some special libraries or information centers which have a large staff, with a number of professional librarians, subject specialists, and a strong support staff, by far the largest number are managed and run by a single person who may or may not have a degree from an accredited library or information school. Some of these small libraries do not even have support staff. The superior to whom the head of these information centers reports is usually not a librarian and often has little or no knowledge of libraries or of what to expect from a librarian. Managers of small information centers are often on their own not only to give reference service but also to perform all the operations of the library.

Professor Tees is on the faculty of the Graduate School of Library Science, McGill University, 3459 McTavish St., Montreal PQ, Canada H3A 1Y1.

© 1986 by The Haworth Press, Inc. All rights reserved.

In this article I will confine myself to discussing small information centers, and I will use the term "special librarian" to refer to the person who runs the small information center and whose most important function is normally that of reference librarian.

QUALIFICATIONS FOR THE JOB

Qualifications for managers of small information centers fall into three basic categories: knowledges, skills, and personal qualities and attitudes. Librarians who have graduated from library schools should have the basic knowledges and skills to work as reference librarians. They may not, however, be prepared to manage the small information center and there are some requirements which are particularly important for these special librarians.

Knowledges

Subject knowledge. The most controversial of the knowledges is the subject knowledge. Is it necessary to have a double master's degree in the subject in which the information center specializes to do effective reference? Many employers prefer a person with a subject specialty to one with skills in information handling, but there is real doubt about the validity of this preference. Unquestionably it is preferable to employ a person with some knowledge of the vocabulary and literature of a field than to have someone with absolutely no familiarity. More and more special librarians are required to do more than simply to answer questions or to provide specific documents for users. They need to understand the material they deal with so that they can select, analyse, evaluate, and package information in a form which will be useful and acceptable to their users. Abstracts, tables, graphs, quotations, and other messaged information are provided by special librarians. This implies a quantity of trust on the part of the user that librarians know what they are doing, and that they are familiar enough with their subjects to be able to package material accurately and clearly.

An experienced librarian will have been able to acquire this subject knowledge on the job, but new librarians will be more effective if they have a good educational background in the subject. However, in most areas it is not extremely difficult to learn enough of a subject to be able to work effectively to select, organize, and retrieve information. A willingness to read, listen, consult, and perhaps take continuing education courses will give new librarians an overall knowledge, especially of the subject vocabulary, to enable them to deal with reference work. What is important is that librarians have a broad general education with a basic knowledge of many subjects so that there is a foundation for further learning. In fact a person with deep knowledge of a very specialized subject may lack the breadth of knowledge that is needed in most information centers.

Knowledge of the literature. Along with knowledge of a subject goes knowledge of its literature. The general reference sources with which all librarians need to be familiar are not enough in most information centers. Literature of different subjects is often produced and organized differently, and special librarians need to be aware of how literature is developed in their own fields and how it can be obtained, organized, and used. Bibliographic tools, whether in hard copy or online, are essential and librarians need a good understanding of the most important data bases and how to use them.

Knowledge of technology. Technology for libraries is a rapidly changing field, and one which is more and more a part of the curriculum of most library schools. Knowledge of the way in which technology affects information and libraries is important for special librarians. With the increase in the use of microcomputers in information centers, special librarians need to be able to find and evaluate software and to use it in information work. In a field which changes as rapidly as information technology, special librarians need to have a basic understanding of what computers can do and be able to assess the value of new developments as they occur. It is easy to be carried away with enthusiasm for each new wave, but prudence dictates a degree of caution which must be based on knowledge.

Skills

Essential to reference librarians in the information center are a number of technical and managerial skills. Hillis L. Griffin, in a paper given at the twentieth annual Clinic on Library Applications of Data Processing held in April 1983 at the University of Illinois, identifies these as: professional skills, background knowledge, keyboard skills, logical and analytical skills, searching, bibliographic organization, computer skills, computers on the job, and management skills.[1]

Personal Skills and Attitudes

Most important for the reference librarian in the information center is the attitude of service to the user. This involves not only the ability to answer questions and provide information on request. It also means keeping in close touch with users and with those in the organization who need information whether they know it or not. It means a proactive attitude toward providing information, visiting potential users in labs and offices, finding out their needs for information, their preferred sources, their proposed projects, in order to be alert to the needs of the future as well as those of the present. The proactive reference librarian provides service by scanning the literature and noticing new items which can be sent to the user, keeping a profile of each user and matching it with the new literature received or reviewed, and keeping in close touch with the changes in the organization so that the information center can change with it and continue to provide the proactive service that is useful. James Matarazzo, in his study of five corporate libraries that were closed by top management,[2] found that the reason for their closing was not that these libraries were ineffectual or were not doing their job; it was because they had not perceived the need to change themselves to serve a changing organization, and because they had not been able to sell themselves to the people in their organization who made the decisions.

Guy St. Clair, writing about the one-person library[3] describes the requirements of the manager of such a library as being self-management, personal affirmation, the ability to say no and to restrict personal work, and the ability to communicate. He says, "In the one-person library, it is essential that the librarian . . . think of himself as a professional. He needs it for his own professional affirmation and also to keep the level of service where it should be." He describes the long list of duties that must be accomplished by the librarian and says, "To do all these jobs and to do them well requires a level of self-management that none of us are taught in graduate school and few of us learn even later. It is easy to say we can manage our time, especially if we are part of a staff and duties are defined; but it is difficult to do it when everything must be done by one person. There are no rules imposed by management, there are no time-sheets, there are no supervisors looking over one's shoulders."

What, then are the qualifications for special librarians in small information centers? They must have knowledge of the special subjects in which they will be working, of the appropriate literature, and of the technology developing in the information field. They need management, communication, and technology skills. They must be self-starters, self-managers, and must be proactive in their service to clients.

Selecting and Hiring the Special Librarian

Librarians have been perceived as passive, service-oriented people who perform useful work in response to requests from users. The very term often used for library clients, "patrons," implies a feudal relationship between librarian and user. The need for dynamic people with managerial as well as information and subject skills is well recognized within the profession but it is not yet well accepted outside. In small information centers where selection is likely to be done by non-librarians, a dynamic personality may not be the first thing the recruiter looks for in the librarian. But it should be as important as the information and subject skills if the librarian in the information center is to be effective, and it is all the more important since the reference librarian is the only person to manage and to provide information.

Selection of the special librarian in the small information center will usually be made by a personnel officer or by the person to whom the special librarian reports, often the head of the research department or an administrative officer. Since these people may be totally unfamiliar with the skills and abilities of the graduate of a library school there is a strong possibility that a quite unqualified person may be selected. A real failure of our profession has been its inability to ensure that recruiters seeking information professionals turn to schools which prepare people to work in information as readily as when seeking lawyers they turn to law schools or when seeking managers they turn to schools of management. The columns of *THE REFERENCE LIBRARIAN* are not the place to inform personnel departments of this matter. A good further step would be the preparation of guidelines for recruiters of information center managers to inform them of the educational background they can expect from library school graduates.

Formal Education of Reference Librarians

Education by library schools for reference service has been discussed at length in the literature. In recent years there has been a change from emphasis on learning about reference sources to emphasis on skills in the reference interview and in online searching strategies. Samuel Rothstein, in an interesting survey of the education of reference librarians, refers to "the welcome shift in scope and emphasis from a narrow concentration on the 'tools' of reference work to a concern with other important matters such as bibliographic structure, search strategy, and, especially, knowing how to deal with the patron."[4] It is still necessary for graduates to be familiar with basic reference sources, but the interpersonal skills needed to understand the needs of the user, and the technical skills to use computerized data bases have become more and more important. William Summers, writing on "Education for reference services"[5] says, "when asked to indicate the most significant changes affecting education for reference service in the past decade, the faculty surveyed for this study indicated the following: (1) a major shift away from a focus on specific tools to a broader focus involving search strategies and a much wider context of information service; (2) a much greater emphasis upon the technological aspects of reference, especially computerized data bases; and (3) an increased emphasis upon the behavioral aspects of information seeking and the processes of human communication." He further states that the three major skills required by reference librarians in the future will be "less knowledge of specific sources and much more knowledge of literatures and their structures," "more substantial knowledge of specific subjects," and "more about users."

Summers is discussing reference service in all types of libraries. When special librarians are asked what they expect of library school graduates, they frequently emphasize the need to know the reference sources and to be able to search online. Herbert S. White and Marion Paris investigated which courses librarians consider most important for students to take in library schools. "Basic Reference" heads the list in almost every type of library. Large and medium-sized special libraries also listed advanced reference, online searching, and database selection among their most highly recommended courses.[6] White and Paris did not include small special libraries in their study.

In a useful article by Carolyn Luck entitled, "Staff training for the information center," she discusses information and referral service in a social service agency.[4] She defines "I & R" service as "linking a person who has a need or problem with a service which can meet the need or solve the problem. The link between the person and what he or she needs is made up of information, and it is this linking process with which we are concerned." Luck is dealing here with linking people with community services, some of which will be available through publications, but many of which are not, and she thinks that many librarians do not recognize that this type of information service requires the same knowledges and skills that are taught to librarians. Luck thinks that librarians bring to this service the traditional skills of organizing and making available large quantities of material, as well as the skill of interviewing, but that many do not recognize that these skills are useable not only with documents but also with all kinds of information in a variety of formats or sources. She says, "the most frequently expressed fear of the inadequacy of librarians is that they do not have the communication skills or the 'humanness' to deal with real problems of real people." She believes that this can and should be taught. Communication of information and ideas in all their forms is what library service is all about. Luck's information center, though differing from other information centers in subject and type of organization, is similar to other centers in business, industry, hospitals, museums, and a host of other organizations in that it links people and information and that the people it links with information have a need which is not related to education and which is not necessarily filled by references to published sources.

The basic education, then, for the reference librarian in the small information center must include not only a knowledge of basic reference sources but also the ability to communicate, the interpersonal skills to understand the needs of the user, whether those needs are for documents or for some other form of linking, and the ability to use computer technology to find information.

On-the-Job Training

Even if special librarians have degrees from an accredited library school, knowledge of appropriate subject specialties, and can meet the need for dynamic management and communication skills, there is much to be learned on a job. Who will do this training?

In the already established small information center, the new librarian is lucky if the former incumbent is on hand for a week or two before the new one is left alone to take over. The former librarian can give the new person at least an overview of the work that has been done, and can introduce him or her to the key members of the staff of the organization and to the needs of users and the sources available to fill them. He or she will also learn the procedures used in the past in the information center. This obviously gives the new librarian a good foundation, especially if the former librarian has been capable and effective.

When there is no previous incumbent, the librarians will have to train themselves, getting help from whatever source is available. It is essential that librarians in small libraries take the initiative to obtain any necessary training they need, and do not wait for someone else to offer it.

What Training is Necessary?

Probably the first thing new librarians need to learn is about the organization in which they work. The new librarian's supervisor will usually be the best person to go to for this kind of information, and will be able to introduce the librarian to potential key users as well as to describe the organization's structure, products, and the political climate within it. Organization charts, annual reports, staff manuals, publications of all kinds emanating from the organization are all indications of the type of work going on within the organization, and the people who are involved. An organizational telephone directory is an invaluable tool to lead librarians to people who will help them to understand the organization better and to people who have needs which might be filled by the information center.

Whether new librarians are subject specialists or not, they will need to get to know the particular literature of use to the organization. This can be done by talking to people, asking them what they use, by looking at what documentation is already in the organization, whether in people's offices and laboratories or in a library or document depository. Reading, naturally, provides a good base on which to build one's special knowledge. A knowledgeable person can give advice, and librarians themselves find suitable books and articles from bibliographic tools in the field. A visit to special libraries serving other similar organizations is of great value, provided the confidentiality of either the visitor or the host is not violated.

Librarians may find that they lack some skill or knowledge that would be useful. There is no lack of courses, workshops, seminars, or lectures on almost any subject. These may be given by local universities or colleges or schools, by library or other associations, either locally or centrally, often during annual or other conferences. The librarian should make management aware of the importance of such training events, and see that there is money in the budget to allow for travel, for conference and workshop fees, and for courses. At the same time, special librarians must be prepared to spend some of their own money in providing their own professional development, and should take advantage of opportunities to keep skills and knowledges up to date.

No professional emerges from school perfectly educated and trained for the present and the future and the professional librarian will be expected to continue to attend courses, to read, and to be in contact with other professionals in order to continue to be on the cutting edge of the profession.

Conclusion

In the small information center, the librarian is above all a reference librarian, but at the same time, is required to be a self-manager who can manage the information center in a professional way, and can identify the information needs of the organization and of the users and link users with whatever type of information is most valuable to them whether in documents or through some other channel. Special librarians should ideally be graduates of library schools, but they must take their further training into their own hands and find ways to learn and keep up-to-date. Since superiors of special librarians are rarely knowledgeable about the operation of information centers or of the capabilities of the librarian, librarians must show evidence of the professional nature of their work, managing effectively as well as providing information both when requested and from their understanding of the needs of the organization. The small information center is fully effective only when the librarian is a dynamic, knowledgeable, professional.

REFERENCES

1. Griffin, Hillis L. "Special librarians face the new technology." In *Professional Competencies—Technology and the Librarian*, edited by Linda C. Smith. Champagne-Urbana, University of Illinois. Graduate School of Library and Information Service, 1983, p. 77-83.
2. Matarazzo, James M. *Closing the Corporate Library: Case Studies in the Decision-Making Process*. New York, Special Libraries Association, 1981.

3. St. Clair, Guy. "The one-person library: an essay on essentials." *Special Libraries*, 67:5/6, May-June 1976, p. 233-238.

4. Rothstein, Samuel. "The making of a reference librarian." *Library Trends*, 31:3 Winter, 1983, p. 375-399.

5. Summers, F. William. "Education for reference service." In *Service Imperative for Libraries*, Littleton, Colorado, Libraries Unlimited, 1982, p. 157-159.

6. White, Herbert S. and Marion Paris. "Employer preferences and the library education curriculum." *Library Quarterly*, 55:1 January 1985, p. 1-33.

7. Luck, Carolyn. "Staff training for the information center." *Drexel Library Quarterly*, 12:1/2 January-April 1976, p. 69-80.

ADMINISTRATION, EVALUATION, AND STAFF TRAINING

The Reference Librarian as Personnel Administrator

William Miller

Personnel administration is simply the management of people at work. It is often referred to as "human resources management," both to stress the point that humans are involved and to indicate that people are generally an organization's most valuable resource. Even in libraries, which are commonly thought of as mere aggregations of books and other materials, we know that salaries and benefits are often the greatest single cost of operation, and that only people can translate the potentially useful store of materials and information into a tool of actual benefit for the average student and scholar.

If people are important to libraries, they are certainly the lifeblood of any Reference Department. When we think about personnel administration in libraries we normally think of the Personnel Librarian function or of high-level administrative supervision. In fact, however, it is usually the Head of the Reference Department (or the individual with equivalent responsibilities) who functions as the most significant personnel administrator in the Library. This individual typically exercises direct supervision over more professional librarians than anyone else in the library, in addition to supervising clerical staff. Consequently, the reference administrator's skill (or lack of skill) as a coach, mentor, motivator, and evaluator will have enormous impact on the long-term development of staff and, through them, of a library's programs. If the reference administrator lacks knowledge, professional awareness, vision, compassion, and the courage to push for change, the forward progress of the entire library will be affected. Even though the management of Reference is in large part a matter of managing people, most of us bring to our first experience as administrators of the reference function no formal training in the field, and it is probable that most

---

Mr. Miller is Acting Dean of Libraries and Learning Resources, Bowling Green State University, Bowling Green, OH 43403.

© 1986 by The Haworth Press, Inc. All rights reserved.

Heads of Reference have never read a textbook on the subject, nor is there much in the literature of librarianship which is likely to be of help. There is no point to complaining about this situation; it is a simple fact of life and one of the many gaps which a Head of Reference must fill in. Most of us will have learned by observation to a certain extent, and will already be somewhat familiar with such processes as selection procedures, employee services, collective bargaining agreements, and continuing education efforts, especially in institutions in which we have previously been employed. More important than the forms of personnel management, however, is the substance of human resources management—the complex matter of communicating with people, understanding them, and motivating them. Such skills can be studied, but probably cannot be learned if there is no innate sympathy for one's fellow human beings.

The position of Head of Reference requires a special set of personnel skills and sensitivities. No other *line* supervisor must work so closely with both the public and the staff. No other line supervisor must so constantly balance the demands of professional, clerical, and student staff with those of the public and the library's administrative regulations. No other line supervisor must constantly be a "dissatisfier" to professional staff, requiring them to work evenings, weekends, and holidays when all other professional staff are relaxing, and advocating the achievement of higher-order goals (such as publication or professional association activity) which may be at best an unwelcome nuisance to many, while at the same time working closely on a daily basis with all staff, remaining on friendly terms with them, and depending upon them to volunteer that extra measure of effort which insures that the unit will function well.

What qualifications do we call for when we hire someone for such a position? The advertisement will generally call for good communication skills and ability to work harmoniously with colleagues and the public, with supervisory experience desired. What we are really looking for in a new Head of Reference is a person who will command the respect of all staff, be adept in all phases of reference work, and be a "people person." At best this person could be expected to have served an apprenticeship as Assistant Head of Reference elsewhere, and will have some good notion of what skills are required. Quite often, however, the individual has no previous administrative experience, and has been promoted by virtue of demonstrated intelligence and previous success as a reference librarian. It is likely (though by no means certain) that the new Head of Reference will gradually learn the personnel portion of what he or she needs to know through a trial-and-error process which involves some combination of good luck, good sense, and some scrambling around to fill in the gaps in knowledge and training. The challenge would seem to be to learn quickly without making so many mistakes along the way that one's credibility with staff is compromised beyond hope of redemption.

LEARNING TO GET ALONG

If the new Head of Reference was an inside candidate, he or she has undoubtedly demonstrated an ability in the past to get along well with staff; indeed, this is often one of the chief qualifications, especially for those chosen in an acting capacity. The individual soon finds, however, that those qualities which enabled him or her to interact well as a peer of the group do not assure success as a supervisor, and indeed may impede that success. Instead of easy participation in normal complaining about policies and administrative actions, the Head of Reference is now an official spokesperson and can be easily compromised by being party to gossip, rumor, or denigration of superiors. Furthermore, the individual is now an administrative superior and enters into an entirely different set of relationships with former equals. Some of the decisions the Head of Reference makes will inevitably be unpopular; the individual must now bear the result of increasingly critical scrutiny and adjust to the relative isolation inherent in a decision-making position.

It may be particularly difficult for the insider to deal with people who were rivals for the position, people who have been long-term antagonists, and those who are senior in tenure and experience and refuse to acknowledge their formerly "inferior" colleague's right to exercise administrative jurisdiction over them. This is especially true in the areas of evaluation and criticism of poor work habits. In short, then, the insider promoted to a Head of Reference situation will usually have to work hard to overcome a variety of handicaps imposed by the existing network of relationships already established with colleagues. It will be the rare individual who is able to take over the reins of a reference department with enough knowledge, assurance, and strength of character to operate as effectively as would be desirable.

Nor is entering the Head of Reference position as an outside candidate free from peril. The insider knows the territory and the personalities involved; the outsider needs to learn both, in addition to all the fine points of institutional procedure which may be necessary to follow. Any unsuccessful inside candidates may be merciless in their judgements, and the rest of the staff may be cool to the outsider who tries to implement new and therefore threatening changes without having had sufficient time to establish credibility and good interpersonal relationships with staff.

NOT THE BEST OF CONDITIONS

Under the best of circumstances, the reference librarian as personnel administrator labors under unenviable conditions. Compare the position, for instance, with that of the Chair of an English Department. This person presides over a group of generally autonomous personalities who may have little regard for the Chair's position. This is understood, at least tacitly, by all. Someone has to do the job, and one unfortunate soul who needs the money or suffers from a sense of duty agrees to undertake it, perhaps in the hope of stepping ultimately into a Deanship. Yet the Chair does not expect to *like* the job, nor does he or she expect the staff to love, honor, or even obey. Indeed, there is usually little that the Chair of an academic department normally expects to accomplish. The structure of the organization is cast into stone; there are few budgetary decisions to make. Personnel evaluation occurs only at tenure decision time, if then. The Chair will assign the course sections and take care of the administrative details which no one else wishes to attend to, but the members of the department remain independent spirits, free to come and go as they choose, and "reporting" largely to no one but themselves.

Take, on the other hand, a supervisor of clerical personnel in a business setting. The employees may or may not like the individual supervisor, but they respect the position. The rules are clear, written, and perhaps mandated by union agreements. The supervisor expects, and has a right to expect, that the employees will report to work on time, produce at certain rates, dress in certain ways, and in general follow all reasonable rules.

Then there is the reference personnel administrator. The professional staff this person supervises may or may not be faculty, in a strict definition, but in any case they claim professional prerogatives of coming and going as they please, exercising personal judgement on how to spend their time, and in general being autonomous. Nevertheless, the person who supervises them has the obligation to make certain that such people produce work in quantity (handouts, database searches, instructional sessions) and according to strict time constraints (e.g., desk duty, work reporting times, and strict accounting of compensatory time taken for evening and weekend hours worked). The Head of Reference, in the academic setting, is a victim of the uncertain status in which librarians find themselves within the faculty context, and the uncertain status in which academic libraries exist within their institutions. Are librarians to be treated as professionals or as clerks? Most often the Head of Reference has to treat them as both, with a range of expectations which gives mixed signals and creates frustration and unhappiness.

This same reference personnel administrator is probably also supervising a small number of clerical staff who are being given a range of tasks from the most menial to those verging on the highly professional. These people may even be working at the reference desk in tandem with librarians, or performing other tasks of a traditionally professional nature, depending upon their backgrounds and competencies. When they are performing in such a complex manner, these clerical staff members need and deserve to be treated with respect and appreciation. They must be treated simultaneously as clerks and as professionals, which involves skill and tact because of the problems it can cause at both ends.

Such an upgrading of status and a broadening in the range of job responsibilities is often welcomed by clerical staff but in turn creates much uncertainty on their part. A clerk is apt to decide that he or she is now equivalent to a librarian, without a full understanding of what the total range of librarians' responsibilities are. A good deal of training and counseling may be necessary as the reference administrator attempts to expand the person's range of responsibility while at the same time reminding them that they still occupy a clerical role also, and that their new position is circumscribed in various ways. The sensitive clerk will easily be offended, especially if it becomes necessary to endure the malevolence or passive resistance offered by librarians unhappy with his or her new role. Nevertheless the Head of Reference has responsibility for the well-being and professional development of *all* staff and must balance everyone's needs and prejudices in light of the greater good of the organization.

THE CLERICAL STAFF ROLE

Librarians, as mentioned above, are very likely to be dismayed at any expansion in the work responsibilities of clerical staff. They are quick to point out, too often with considerable justification, that they already lack sufficient clerical support, and that there is little understanding at the top echelons of the library about why they might need such support. So why take clerical staff away from existing duties in order to expand into professional territory? Nevertheless in order to provide job satisfaction for clerical staff, carry out new programs, cope with pressing personnel shortages, and maximize the existing professionals' time, the Head of Reference may wish to use clerical staff for tasks formerly performed by librarians. This upgrading may well be a threat to some insecure librarians, and others sincerely believe that no compromise in the level at which tasks are currently performed is morally justifiable. For his or her trouble and willingness to innovate, therefore, the Head of Reference may expect to earn the dislike of many among the professional staff, who may look for appropriate opportunities to sabotage the new program of activity.

Perhaps the most difficult situation which the reference administrator faces is the necessity of dealing with the diversity in levels of both motivation and competence among all staff, and the challenge of melding all people in the unit into one homogeneous group. Some of the clerical staff may clearly be more capable and energetic than some of the librarians; the reference personnel administrator will want to provide such people with challenges while at the same time recognizing the limitations inherent, as a result of education or of institutional salary and labor agreements, in what such people can be expected to do. Among the librarians, some will be high-energy self-starters who perhaps need to be counseled to slow down because they are burning themselves out, carrying a larger share of the workload than their more quiescent colleagues, and carrying a larger share of the unit's effort than they can ultimately sustain. The Head of Reference must avoid the temptation to take advantage of these hard workers and use their herculean efforts as a way out of avoiding difficult personnel confrontations with those who work less diligently.

The latter, whether clerical or professional, constitute what is surely one of the reference personnel administrator's most universal problems. In his recent editorial "The Crisis in Academic Reference Work," James Rettig decried the fact that too many reference librarians leave the field after several years of experience.[1] The average Head of Reference would probably wish to amend Rettig's feelings to state that too many *good* reference librarians leave the field after several years, to go on to administration or some other kind of work. The deadwood, unfortunately, seem to remain with us forever. Tenured or with some comparable kind of job security which makes them impossible to be rid of, they seem like a curse on the land, to be endured but never changed.

What has most typically occurred is that a double standard has come into existence over the years in most reference departments. Everyone expects that the overachievers should continue to overachieve, take extra desk hours and weekend assignments, and generally take responsibility for making sure that things actually function properly. Everyone expects, on the other hand, that the underachievers—who have been babied, protected, indulged, and given *pro forma* positive evaluations for so long—will continue to underachieve. Indeed, this situation has typically achieved such permanence and seeming legitimacy through long practice that it seems like cruel and unusual punishment to subject non-achievers and underachievers to the same standards and expectations which we apply to more productive staff.

PERFORMANCE EVALUATION

Nevertheless, that is exactly the problem which reference personnel administrators must grapple with or fail in any attempt to move the unit and the library itself forward. The anvil here is performance evaluation, usually avoided when possible or, when not possible, conducted as painlessly and perfunctorily as possible. Unfortunately, however, it is not really possible to motivate staff without continual and sometimes critical evaluation and feedback on their performance. All staff, but particularly those who are thought of as marginal or poor performers, must have a written set of mutually-agreed upon expectations. One should not make the mistake of assuming that evaluation of such people is necessarily useless and hopeless because they must obviously know what the problems are and are resolutely intent on avoiding the solutions. Typically, for a variety of reasons, they are unaware of how others perceive them, and are quite shocked to realize that it is they who are considered the source of the unit's underperformance problems.

Indeed, one thing a reference personnel administrator learns if he or she confronts the poor performers of the department during an evaluation or at some other point is that they believe themselves to be, in fact, the best performers, albeit unsung and unappreciated. Amazing as it might seem to the supervisor, the employee who is regularly out sick or otherwise unavailable twenty-five percent of the time may well be quite taken aback at the notion that there is anything wrong with such behavior. The employee has probably not realized the effect that such absences have on the desk schedule and the work schedules of the other individuals in the unit, nor has the employee realized the resentment which others probably feel as a result of the increased burden this person's performance has forced them to carry. Such employees, whether clerical or professional, need and deserve to be told what the administrator perceives the problems to be, and what would constitute acceptable performance. They need specific goals and deadlines, along with periodic evaluation sessions to gauge progress.

There is no guarantee that performance will improve as a result of evaluation.[2] The task of motivating is a complex one which depends on much more than an honest awareness of the facts. Supervisors have no control over employees' personal lives, and may have little success at engaging in behavior modification. Some individuals by their nature appear to lack drive, industry, or other traits usually considered desirable on the job, and for other individuals the motivation and satisfaction they need and do in fact strive for is associated with areas unrelated to their work-lives. Such limitations, however, do not absolve the supervisor from the obligation to attempt to motivate people and ameliorate unsatisfactory situations. With time, patience, and perseverence, some underachievers *will* shape up and make modest but real contributions to the organization. If they do, it may be possible to move ahead with some new initiatives or redistribute the workload in some fairer fashion. And, in at least some cases, anguish and tears will be replaced by gratitude as employees long given up for dead are rejuvenated, with consequent increases in self-esteem as well as in productivity.

ROLE MODELS NEEDED

Closely allied to the need for performance evaluation is the need for mentoring. Professional staff in particular need a role model and need encouragement to become professionally involved. The Head of Reference functions as a role model willy-nilly—if he or she never publishes, does not become involved with professional association activities, and fails to keep abreast of new technological and professional developments, it will be pointless to urge others in the unit to do so unless they are intent on doing so already. This need to advocate professional development has library-wide implications, for the simple reason that, as pointed out above, a significant number of the library's professional staff are likely to be in the reference area. If they are not growing professionally, trying new things and experimenting with new services, they are likely to stagnate and look elsewhere for their satisfaction and motivation. If their growth is stunted and their enthusiasm wanes, library services will suffer and the public will be quick to notice and complain.

Were the reference administrator working in a business situation, of course, many of these problems would be more easily solvable. Non-productive employees could be terminated. Programs which were not profitable would be eliminated, and employee bonuses could encourage innovative thinking and acting. Increases in productivity would mean increases in profit, some of which could be put toward new staffing to cope with increases in workload. Just the opposite situation obtains in libraries however. Reference departments do not operate in a capitalist economy. Non-productive workers cannot be shipped out if they refuse to shape up. Increases in workload occasioned by the rise of new programs in instruction and database searching do not lead to increases in staff. The reward for work well done is more work.[3]

This artificial situation places the reference administrator in a precarious position. He or she advocates change, growth, new ideas. However, as the work increases, expands, and becomes more challenging and complex, the best performers begin to wilt, and the worst rebel. All look to their Head of Reference for relief, but that person can do little to provide it. Institutional budgets do not allow for increases in staff proportional to increasing workload, or increases in equipment which would allow existing staff to work more efficiently, nor is there much ability or interest from above in rearranging library priorities to shift resources to reference functions. Indeed, the library's upper administration may be depressingly unsympathetic to the problem, refusing to recognize the pressures which beset public service staff.

This overload crisis is a relatively new but pressing problem for reference administrators. If staff attribute the problem to their administrative leader, that person may become isolated from all constituencies and lose the good-will and staff support previously cultivated and merited. The reference administrator who faces this problem will find that addressing it is no simple task. It is much easier to introduce new library programs than it is to curtail them; the same administration which disparages complaints about overwork refuses to allow the department to reduce its own workload. The same staff members who have consistently refused to increase their own personal contributions now see the wisdom of their ways in the fatigue of their more energetic colleagues. The same staff who have been the enthusiastic "doers" may become hesitant or even cynical and pull back from commitment. The reference administrator, if not careful, can become the individual left twisting in the wind with little support from those either above or below in the hierarchy if he or she attempts to continue to press for the unrealistic or impossible, regardless of how desirable these may seem.

RECIPE FOR SUCCESS

What, then, is the most likely recipe for success for a reference librarian in the role of personnel administrator today? The *sine qua non* would be to take the measure of all staff, and to judge from that measure the likelihood that current programs can be improved, and the wisdom of instituting new programs. It might be the better part of valor for a new Head of Reference to spend the first year of incumbency in establishing close personal relationships, rather than in charging ahead with insufficiently-considered new program initiatives, however desirable such programs might be in the abstract. During this period of time the Head of Reference should pitch in to all of the department's programs and gain respect as one who is capable of performing all the tasks called for, and as one who is not only willing to do, but who also actually does all that he or she would ask the members of the department to do, and more.

The ultimate goal of a Head of Reference should be to create a climate for change which is informed by his or her knowledge of professional developments. The supervisor's objectives need to be ambitious but realistic; the supervisor's treatment of staff needs to be even-handed, firm, and consistent. The supervisor should expect to lead by example to a far greater extent than by decree. If such a climate has been created, the more highly motivated staff will be nurtured and the least professional will be brought along in a relatively non-threatening atmosphere which will probably maximize the degree to which they will participate in the work of the unit.

Needless to say, personnel administration is only one of the challenges the Head of Reference faces, and the active role for a reference personnel administrator outlined here is an ideal which can only be achieved by brave individuals of strong character who are willing to undergo unpleasantness of many kinds and maintain high leadership profiles. Of course library directors and personnel librarians face many of the same issues as do Heads of Reference. The difference, however, is that the Head of Reference must in effect live with the people he or she is also "managing," and does not have the luxury of issuing edicts from a main office, or of treating staff like chess pieces, without having to face the immediate personal consequences of decisions. Therein lies the real challenge of personnel administration in the reference setting.

REFERENCES

1. "The Crisis in Academic Reference Work," *Reference Services Review* 12 (Fall 1984):13-14.
2. Richard P. Calhoon, in *Personnel Management and Supervision*, notes that "even in management positions, motivating toward greater effort is a difficult task. Engineers and scientists . . . are especially 'troublesome' to motivate" (New York: Appleton Century Crofts, 1967), p. 198.
3. For a fuller discussion of this topic see my article "What's Wrong With Reference" in *American Libraries* 15 (May 1984): 303-306, 321-322.

Evaluating the Reference Librarian

Sara B. Sluss

Performance appraisal, performance evaluation, annual evaluation, self-evaluation; all are labels for processes which occur on some regular basis, by a more or less formal method, and are prepared for a variety of reasons in many organizations. Organizations use evaluation processes to document the work performance of their employees. These processes can be rigidly defined and instituted with quantifiable standards against which each employee will be judged. Or the process may be very informal—a brief, comfortable conference whose outcome may be based primarily on the employer's or supervisor's subjective response to the person being evaluated. Such appraisals may take place on a regular schedule; such as at the end of the calendar year or academic year, on or near an employee's "anniversary" date, or prior to an employee being considered for promotion or salary increases. The performance appraisal may be designed to serve any one or any combination of functions, such as: to change or modify inappropriate or inferior work behavior, to initiate and routinize dialogues between employer and employee concerning perceptions of quality and quantity of performance, to assess potential of the employee as regards training and development opportunities, to determine appropriate compensation level for the employee, or to provide documentation of work behavior in cases where disciplinary action may be warranted. Evaluation may be completed solely by direct supervisors, or information may be elicited from colleagues, clients, users, students, or from someone subordinate to the employee being evaluated. The process may begin with an oral and/or written self-evaluation followed by an oral and/or written evaluation by the employer. The employee may have an opportunity to respond to the evaluation. The permutations and ramifications are endless.

The author is at the Staley Library, Milliken University, Decatur, IL 62522.

© 1986 by The Haworth Press, Inc. All rights reserved.

A "FAIR" EVALUATION

There is a tendency among persons involved in any personnel evaluation process, either as evaluator or as "evaluatee" to equate fairness with objectivity. In other words, the parties agree that the more objective this process can be made, the less subjective the evaluation, and hence, the more "fair" it becomes. Each party tends to objectify the process; the evaluatee wanting some method which would disallow or deter negative subjective judgments or extraneous comments on non-work related activities or behavior, and the evaluator wishing for some formula that would simplify this task and perhaps lessen the burden of his/her personal responsibility. If only performance could be measured exactly, if only output measures could be applied to all tasks for all positions, if only quality control standards could be developed for all employment situations. . . .

Is it best to attempt to objectify or quantify all aspects of performance? If forced to quantify the unquantifiable, doesn't the organization run the risk of developing arbitrary or even meaningless standards for performance? Some portion of an evaluation system may, by necessity, be objective or have some numerical standard applied to it. An employee may be hired to produce a minimum number of widgets in a specified time. That employee may also be judged on personal traits that do not have a direct effect on the number of widgets he/she produces, but may effect the quality of work life and performance of the other widget makers in the firm. For most employees performance is not, and can not be, restricted entirely to quantifiable measures (regardless of whether it is the number of widgets, items cataloged, reference questions answered), but also to a less discrete measure which requires the evaluation of the quality of performance, such as the ability to interact congenially with other workers or clients, quality of cataloging, or satisfaction of patrons with reference information supplied. Personality traits which affect performance and users' perceptions of quality of services provided are among the factors that make performance appraisal an inexact science at best.

RELUCTANCE TO EVALUATE

In his article on performance appraisals, Stanley P. Hodges forwarded a number of reasons for reluctance among personnel to devote the necessary time and effort to the evaluation process.[1] The reasons can be diverse and range from unwillingness among managers to take time away from "more productive" tasks to a feeling among employees that such evaluations have no real effect. These reasons may stem from a perception among employees that their evaluator's decisions and recommendations may be disregarded or over-ridden by those administrators at the next higher level. Employees may not have much faith in the process if they feel that the manager has already made decisions based on perceptions unrelated to actual performance and that the formal performance appraisal is, in fact, a ruse used by the manager to give the appearance of fairness where little exists. A manager who feels that performance appraisal is not a productive task not only misunderstands the reasons for the process, but perhaps has misunderstood her/his own role in the process. Middle managers may also have concerns about how evaluations of the staff can be used as a tool to evaluate their own supervisory skills. Middle managers may be reluctant to give negative appraisals of subordinates, even when such appraisals may be in order, if they fear that top level management might blame them (rightly or wrongly) for their subordinate's poor performance.

The problems of evaluating reference librarians are multitudinous and may not be entirely a result of the work itself. Librarians may have been reluctant to open themselves up to a process which had traditionally been "limited to the production line and to junior management in the business world, and to clerical positions in the world of libraries."[2] Librarians may also have resisted traditional evaluation techniques because of the perspectives that they bring to the work that they do. Librarians, like teachers, are in the somewhat unusual position of having spent many years as users of the products and services that they now offer. How unlike the corporate world where frequently managers are brought in directly from the university or are recruited from managerial pools in other corporations, and may have never used the corporation's products previously, nor had any experience as a rank and file worker in that firm. Academic librarians may feel hesitant about seeking formal evaluative input from library users since those users have a limited understanding of programs and services. Academic library users may be unable to understand or unwilling to accept the compromises that are necessary when librarians divide limited budgets and services among a wide variety of users who represent a plethora of needs.[3]

There has also been institutional unwillingness, particularly in academic settings, to apply the same standards to the evaluation of librarians as has been applied to the remainder of the academic community. Oftentimes in those settings, librarians have been forced into existing evaluation schemes and ranking systems. These schemes, which may be imperfect even for the segment of the community—be it full time teaching faculty or administrative staff—for which they were designed, become doubly so when squeezed and stretched to accommodate persons whose roles within the community can't be defined entirely as either teaching in the narrow sense or as support staff.

Within some academic settings librarians may have had the opportunity to develop their own evaluation schemes for internal use, but still may be subject to faculty promotion rules and regulations. This model is frequent in those institutions in which librarians are considered "almost faculty" and are assigned faculty rank or equivalent rank, are given some of the responsibilities of faculty (i.e., committee assignments), and may or may not be eligible for benefits, such as tenure, that accrue to teaching faculty. The criticism that teaching faculty have of promotion and tenure committees, which are usually composed of their teaching colleagues, are that teaching methods vary significantly among the disciplines, that what may constitute substantial scholarly activity in one field may seem inconsequential to someone in another discipline, and that it may be very difficult for faculty outside of a particular discipline to make competent decisions concerning the quality of these activities. It is no wonder that some librarians view the promotion and/or tenure process with trepidation. If teaching faculty can not reconcile differences across the disciplines, then can they clearly understand the difficulties in determining the quality of service offered by a professional librarian?

PROBLEMS OF EVALUATING SERVICES

The difficulties inherent in the evaluation of reference services and personnel are the selfsame problems for any service profession. A reference librarian can not be evaluated wholly on the number of hours spent at an information desk, the number of questions answered correctly, or any other measure of quantity. The quality of service or performance in the role must be determined, and herein the difficulty lies. A typical day in the life of the generic reference librarian could consist of any combination of the following: reference desk assignment; bibliographic instruction; collection development; supervision of support staff or student assistants; on-line data retrieval; research and writing; serving on or chairing library or other institutional committees, or on the committees of professional organizations. A reference librarian may be assigned interlibrary loan duties, work a brief but regular stint in technical services, may do local indexing, prepare bibliographies, assist in card catalog maintenance, plan programs, put up displays, or act as liaison to some segment of the community. The variations on this theme are limitless. Within a particular institution these tasks can be formally or informally weighted and prioritized. Some evaluation procedure for any one of these tasks may be in place. Surveys may be devised to shed some light on user satisfaction with reference services; however, these usually do not evaluate the quality of service offered by a particular librarian, but reflect the users' perceptions of the reference staff in general. These surveys may, in fact, be a better evaluation of collections or technical services than an assessment of reference services and personnel. In a formal classroom setting students can evaluate bibliographic instruction, whether it is the "one shot" variety or a separate course. For most reference librarians, this instruction is at most a few hours each week, so although such evaluations may be reliable and institutionally acceptable, they evaluate only a small portion of the reference librarian's total responsibilities. What the evaluator is confronted with is a multi-faceted service position with tasks which will be weighted uniquely according to institutional needs and that will require a wide variety of "people" skills as well as technical skills. What is needed is a system by which the person performing these tasks can be routinely and systematically evaluated according to the quality of the products and services. The process may also need to be communicated to and clarified for another administrative level or body (academic administrators, promotion and tenure committees, trustees, etc.) which may not be well acquainted with the day-to-day responsibilities of the reference librarian.

LAMA GUIDELINES

The Library Administration Management Association, a division of the American Library association, published in 1979 a guide to personnel performance appraisal. The document briefly outlines the goals of performance appraisal, basic features that should be included in any appraisal program, and the factors that determine a successful performance appraisal. The guide states that the formulation of individual performance goals, along with the documentation of the functions and tasks of the position and a determination or definition of performance standards, are the bases for performance appraisal.[4] Guidelines developed by the Association of Research Libraries for formulating these individual performance goals recommend that " . . . individual performance goals should be quantifiable whenever possible . . .," but do also make clear that " . . . virturally all library goals will require some degree of qualitative evaluation, and that human judgments will of necessity remain an important part of the review process."[5] The qualitative evaluation is the most important factor in appraising the effectiveness of a reference librarian since very few reliable or meaningful quantitative factors exist for those services. The LAMA document does not provide a completely developed system, and consequently, does not provide specitic methods or information concerning implementation of these quidelines, nor do they examine the potential problems of implementation. What follows is a prescription for executing the guidelines, specifically addressing the reference librarian in an academic setting.

DOCUMENTING TASKS AND FUNCTIONS

The first step in the performance appraisal process must be the development of a detailed written job description. The existing job description for the reference librarian may be as vague as the classified ads for position openings: reference desk duty xx hours each week, one night per week, occasional weekend assignments; supervises a staff of xx students and xx FTE; responsibilities include collection development, bibliographic instruction, and on-line searching in the field of xxx. The job description used for the performance appraisal program must be a detailed, creative, and vital working document that presents not only the major foci of the position, but some definition of and methods for achieving the major points. The reference librarian's major responsibility will be reference services, but these services and peripheral activities could be documented within the job description as illustrated in the following examples:

1. *Hours at Reference Desk.* Should address general expectations concerning hours on reference duty, as opposed to hours devoted to other facets of the job. Should note specifically evening and/or weekend assignments.

2. *Levels of Service.* *If* institutional policy dictates (implicity or explicitly) that reference service levels vary according to differences in user groups, then these groups should be identified and described, and service differences reflected in the job description. Example: Reference Librarian A will perform online searches for teaching faculty and graduate assistants.
3. *Collection Development Responsibilities.* Should describe what subject areas or phases of collection development that person is responsible for, i.e., selection, weeding, inventory, policy setting, evaluation, resource sharing, etc.
4. *Bibliographic Instruction.* Should describe formal and/or informal programs the person is responsible for or participates in. Methods for accomplishment of this service, i.e., preparation of pathfinders, classroom presentations, etc., should be outlined.
5. *Supervisory Responsibilities.* Should describe the extent of supervision expected. Is the supervision needed the day-to-day overseeing of student assistants who will perform tasks which need very little instruction, or is the supervision of clerical staff, or other professional librarians, or some combination of these? Will the reference librarian be monitoring these persons on their performance of prescribed tasks, then reporting to another person who administers that department or division? Or will the reference librarian be expected to assign tasks, monitor their completion, develop goals and objectives with subordinates, and finally evaluate these persons?
6. *Lines of Authority.* For each general task outlined in the reference librarian's job description it should be made explicit to whom he/she reports or with whom he/she works to complete the task. Example: Reference Librarian B will develop and execute a formal bibliographic instruction program in consultation with the Head of the Reference Division.

GOALS DEVELOPMENT

The preparation of this detailed job description to be used for appraisal should be done in close consultation between the supervisor and the reference librarian. Once such a document is developed and deemed acceptable to the parties involved, the next step is the formulation of individual performance goals for that particular person. For the librarian new to the institution or to the position it will be necessary for the supervisor to be considerably more directive about goals development than it would be for a more established librarian who would have a better sense of what can be accomplished within a particular evaluation period and who would have a clearer understanding of institutional goals. It may be fruitful to have the new librarian work with a more experienced staff member who is in a position of similar responsibility to develop a rough draft of goals that reflect institutional and departmental needs. Examples of goals and objectives which could be developed for the reference librarian are:

1. Responsibility: Collection Development—Reference.
   Goal: Improve selection procedures.
   Objective: Develop a Reference Purchase Policy File which would document decisions made on certain (costly) reference items. The file will include citations to and notes about reviews, comments made about examination copies, etc.
   Goal: Inventory.
   Objective: Will plan and execute complete inventory of reference collection for Summer 19xx.
   Goal: Develop weeding policies.
   Objective: Study weeding policies and procedures at similar institutions. Prepare written policy statement.
2. Responsibility: Bibliographic Instruction.
   Goal: Improve teaching methods.
   Objective: Consult with University Teaching Consultant. Invite Consultant to observe class and make comments.
   Goal: Increase number of presentations (one-shot instruction).
   Objective: Send "reminders" to faculty that reference librarians are available for classroom presentations on research strategies.

These individual performance goals should be developed to be accomplished or to be performed on a continuing basis through the next evaluation period. Long-range and continuing goals and objectives will obviously be included—weeding, improvement of instruction, continuing education, etc.—but short-term and specific goals should be included as well:

1. Responsibility: Collection Development—Sciences.
   Goal: Improve quality of chemistry collection.

Objective: Evaluate chemistry collection using core collection lists such as *Books for College Libraries* and *Guidelines and Suggested Title List for Undergraduate Chemistry Libraries*. Concentrate on selection and weeding in this area.
2. Responsibility: General Reference Services.
Goal: Updating Library Pathfinders collection.
Objective: Evaluate amount of use, revise pathfinders as needed, prepare new pathfinders in areas X1, X2, and X3.
3. Responsibility: Supervision of Support Staff.
Goal: Improve managerial skills through continuing education.
Objective: Identify and attend one library-oriented management workshop during the next year.

INFORMAL CONFERENCE

Throughout the appraisal period the parties involved should independently examine and, in an informal conference, discuss difficulties and successes with the goals. This will give the reference librarian an opportunity to inform the supervisor if any goals/objectives are "unachievable" or were overly ambitious and may require revision. It will give the supervisor an opportunity to offer advice or assistance, or merely check on progress. These informal conferences should be scheduled frequently and regularly, perhaps set to some institutional "clock," such as by quarters or semesters. If the conferences are not scheduled on a regular basis, there is a likelihood, especially when all else has been operating "status quo," that the employee will feel hesitant about opening communication channels and broaching problems with the supervisor if difficulties do develop later.

FORMAL EVALUATION CONFERENCE

Before the formal evaluation conference at the end of the appraisal period the reference librarian should submit to the supervisor a written, point by point evaluation of how each goal and objective has been approached and achieved or what progress has been made. This written evaluation should address any factors encountered that influenced how successful or unsuccessful she/he was in the performance of particular duties. The reference librarian should also begin formulating a tentative goals and objectives statement or individualized "contract" for the subsequent appraisal period. The actual evaluation conference should be scheduled to allow sufficient uninterrupted time for both parties to make comments, criticisms, and suggestions, and to ask questions without any pressure. The supervisor should always make available to the employee his/her own written evaluation. The negotiation and prioritization of goals and objectives for the next evaluation period is the last segment of the formal evaluation conference. Negotiation is a key concept in this process. The supervisor should not design and set goals without discussing them with the employee, nor should the employee expect that his/her own goals and objectives will in all cases fit the needs of the institution or the department, or the expectations of the supervisor.

TRUSTING THE PROCESS

There must exist within the institution and between the individuals involved in the performance evaluation a considerable "trust factor" for the program to work successfully. If the employee does not have faith that the system works fairly, and suspects that it is being abused by supervisors, top level administration, or even by peers, then the system is prone to failure. Evaluation programs of all types can be abused and this one is no exception. The process can be violated by supervisors who set up or suggest "unachievable" goals—a poor manager's method for discouraging and discarding unwanted employees. There also may be supervisors who will take a "percentage" approach to such a system, i.e., six of ten goals achieved equals poor performance, eight of ten goals achieved equals average performance, all ten goals achieved equals superior performance. This short-sighted approach does not take under consideration the abilities of the individual employee or the overall difficulty or creativity of the goals. If such abuses by superiors exist, or if employees suspect that they exist, then other forms of misuse will undoubtedly occur. Employees will learn to compose less than ambitious or unchallenging goals, perceiving that if they can show successful completion of all stated goals each review period that they will be evaluated as "superior" employees. In such circumstances not only does the institution suffer because no one puts effort, energy, or imagination into the goal setting process, but each individual suffers because there is no institutional incentive which encourages creativity and professional growth. There are situations in which both the supervisor and the employee enter into the performance appraisal program in good faith only to discover that top level administrators do not consider the results seriously or even disregard comments and recommendations issuing from the process. Supervisors and employees in such situations can become demoralized, will expend very little energy on what seems to be a meaningless task, and will eventually find "more productive" tasks to devote their time to.

EVALUATING QUALITY

The key question for supervisor and reference librarian alike is: What kinds of goals and objectives for services reflect a "quality" reference librarian: Is a "good" librarian one who has a high percentage of "hits" or who, according to users or to some observer, has answered most questions put to him/her correctly? Who reacts to each approach to the reference desk non-judgmentally and with enthusiasm? And what of the relative merit of a reference librarian who, when requested to instruct students in methods of research, responds with appropriately designed strategies and instructional materials? These are all minimum quality requirements and are all hallmarks of a good reference librarian. But is "good" good enough?

SATISFACTORY VS. SUPERIOR

In the development of goals and evaluation of performance both parties in the appraisal program must distinguish between satisfactory and superior performance or between reactive and proactive reference services. The distinctions will aid the evaluator to distinguish between the librarian who is responding adequately and correctly to achieve institutional and departmental goals and to fulfill the informational needs of the individual, and the librarian who anticipates, investigates, and develops products and services which can be marketed to the university community. The former is a "reactive" librarian, and the latter is "proactive." A competent reactive librarian is an asset to the institution; the proactive librarian is a blessing. Such people can dramatically increase the visibility and status of the library within the academic community. The proactive librarian won't wait at the desk, surrounded by the latest in reference sources, but will find methods of marketing new reference books. As a result of studying course outlines or analyzing course descriptions in the university catalog, the proactive librarian will be able to anticipate where and when new reference materials could be used and can notify teaching faculty. A pre-printed card or memo can be designed to inform faculty of new reference books, new editions, or other library materials which may be of use in their classes or by their students. Brief comments can be appended or even photocopies of tables of content or introductions can be attached which elaborate and illustrate how the reference book could be incorporated. To simplify this notification process the reference librarian can design a file (rotary, card, or computerized) of cross-references matching faculty to topical interests. In developing this file, the librarian should keep in mind that faculty interests usually far exceed the content of the courses they teach, especially at smaller institutions where a faculty member may teach a broad spectrum of courses, but spend little actual course time on the subfields in which they specialize. The librarian will want to discover and document these research interests through either informal day-to-day contact with faculty or some more systematic method of formal interviews or surveys of faculty. The librarian should not neglect the needs of administrative staff and part time faculty who may have less information about library resources available to them than would the full time teaching faculty. The proactive librarian can increase the visibility of the library by notifying members of the university community at the beginning of the semester or of the year and reminding them of what services are available: assistance in designing library research assignments, bibliographic instruction, on-line searching, preparation of bibliographies, etc. The superior librarian must be forward-thinking, anticipating the needs of the university community, rather than merely responding to needs as they are expressed.

REFERENCES

1. Stanley P. Hodge, "Performance Appraisals: Developing a Sound Legal and Managerial System." *College and Research Libraries*, 44 (July 1983), p. 235.
2. H. Rebecca Kroll, "Beyond Evaluation: Performance Appraisal as a Planning and Motivational Tool in Libraries." *Journal of Academic Librarianship*, 9 (March 1983), p. 27.
3. *User Surveys and Evaluation of Library Services*. Washington: Association of Research Libraries, Office of Management Studies, 1981, (Spec kit; 71), (from introduction).
4. *Performance Appraisal*. Chicago: Association of College and Research Libraries, 1980. (CLIP Note # 1-80), pp. 125-132.
5. Ibid, p. 131.

Time Management for Information Services

Bill Bailey

How best to utilize the forty hour week in the Information Services (IS) division of an academic library requires astute planning and enlightened backing by administration. When IS's "raison d'être" is to teach the intricacies of the library to students the entire work week could be spent at the Information Desk. But this numbing posture accomplishes only one end which is to demonstrate that IS librarians visibly serve the public. There are other behind-the-scene facets to teaching the library. Preparation underscores performance and the IS librarian must have quiet moments for study. The desire or mandate to engage in scholarly activities also necessitates time away from the Information Desk. Forty hours a week, or any disproportionate amount, bridled there decreases productivity and hastens burnout. This eclipsing situation can be avoided through time management. First, the individual must exhibit the requisite discipline to achieve the ordinary and beyond. Second, the work week has to be restructured to place greater emphasis on professionalism. The two when dovetailed can completely remake IS.

THE CORPORATE CLOCK

In the world of business time management persists as a much deliberated concept. Where time equates with money and every minute counts, employee theft of the precious commodity debilitates any organization. A look at how business handles time offers insight of use to IS.

David W. Nicastro repeats the joke that the ideal executive is the one who goes to work clutching a list of eleven things to do, and returns home with a new list of fourteen plus the original eleven.

Mr. Bailey is at the Newton Gresham Library, Sam Houston State University, Huntsville, TX 77341.

© 1986 by The Haworth Press, Inc. All rights reserved.

Not wanting to live the joke, Nicastro endorses three axioms to follow when managing people and time. The three are: People are better than you think, equipment should enhance the operation—not vice versa, and pressure of time is a valuable ally.[1]

Applying the axioms to IS comes easily. Everyone on the staff can contribute something of value no matter what talents possessed; never rule out a person to delegate to for reasons of misperceived indifference or incompetence. There are self-starters, and then there are those who have to be nudged. The equipment axiom is especially intriguing now that academic libraries have launched headfirst into the computer age. The on-line catalog has to be up and purring always once the card catalog has been removed; down-time is its nemesis. Optical disks and other vernal services will revolutionize academic libraries. But will the death of the book and the blistering delivery of information rush everyone out of the library? Will we evolve into mere convenience stores with little or no distinction among us? The third axiom, pressure of time, appears irrelevant given the slow pace of Academe. Daily Academe does not "make the big deal" to skyrocket the company. Yet daily an infusion of pressure can result in marked productivity. IS should set up deadlines. Late computer searches and forgotten telephone queries are intolerable. Projects considered indefinitely and carried over from one semester to another are glorious time wasters.

Hardly in need of mention, other time wasters are legion. Warren Keith Schilit recites the most prolific: excessive meetings, visitors, telephone interruptions, fuzzy objectives, personal disorganization, unclear roles, and poor communication. To control them, Schilit suggests: get organized, clarify objectives, and establish priorities. Familiar enough antidotes, though he goes on to advance a golden one. It is, try to examine a single piece of paper once, comment on it, then file it away where it can be found another day. Other of his advisements are: eschew perfectionism, recognize productive hours sealing them off from interruptions, and break up a large job into smaller ones.[2]

Academic librarians seem always to be in meetings. "Tied up" in one is often a literal phrase. Too frequent and lengthy meetings invite lethargy and show a lack of direction and decision-making. Paper shufflers prone to minute scrutiny fits IS and other of the academic librarians. All the more reason to consent to Schilit's golden rule—examine a single piece of paper once. The imposing job pared down to smaller ones looms large as sage advice. For instance, subject specialists should weed their own discipline areas of the collection and should develop their own part of the vertical file. To assign all of either job to one IS librarian would be too much.

General managers who are successful, according to John P. Kotter, devote most of their time to talking with employees—often as much as 90% of the day. The GM's converse about everything under the sun. They ask probing questions but carefully side-step any commitments. They behave in a "reactive mode" and try to limit each chat to around ten minutes per employee. In this diagnostic manner the GM's listen to the heartbeat of the organization and are better able to prescribe for its ills.[3]

Now what of this apparent gadflying about can IS copy? Certainly in a gesture of friendship and to assess department morale, talk with staff compensates. But to visit full-time is in itself a bona fide time waster, and the wonder is how business can afford to indulge executive quidnuncs? A display of favoritism, a lapsing into pettiness, a fracturing of concentration are a few of the natural by-products of the quick chat. Employed sparingly the canvassing of staff concerns is beneficial. A day in court usually clears up problems after which time and energy can be channeled toward accomplishment.

THE IS CLOCK

Leaving business, time management has engendered some interest in the academic library world, though preoccupation with it has not been as pronounced. Library literature speaks to the fact that IS librarians drown under waves of work. Students bearing questions arrive non-stop, teaching faculty call in riddling like a sphinx, and every wanted book has vanished. The Head of IS is even worse off, what with administrative labors Hercules would have fled from. A good deal of circumnavigating and assassinating time seems to be the picture.

It is amiss for IS not to incorporate time management into the melee. The job at hand, i.e., answering questions, is not the only demand IS should satisfy. A full range of scholarly ventures, forever dreamed of, awaits the first move. Absorption in the minutiae of IS is not praiseworthy but foolish. Therefore, clerical duties must be delegated, repetitive tasks dissected for removable parts, and education continued to improve knowledge so that answers come readily. A few changes can bank a lot of time.

AN IMMODEST PROPOSAL

The climate in academic libraries today favors gainful time management. Faculty status for most, higher degreed personnel, proven bibliographic instruction programs, and a spate of outstanding publication have each one elevated the academic librarian. In light of this new repute, twenty hours of work at the Information Desk and twenty off is the correct allotment for IS staff. Too much intrinsic work must be undertaken to stack up reference librarians in one place. The ceiling of twenty hours on desk duty results in a fresher mental outlook, and frustration does not mount because the other half of the week enjoins scholarship which revivifies desk duty.

If IS is not centralized but decentralized scattering librarians, then centralization should be considered. Decentralization has seen its day. In effect it established special libraries within the library replete with individual administrative, down to clerical, duties. Shopkeeping ate up all the time and librarians competed unhealthily to manifest the best shop. Decentralization might still have its attractions, but not to outweigh those of centralization. More tangible work can be compassed when the reference faculty resides in one collegial area. Immediate consultation occurs, absences present no problem, and the opportunity to master the entire reference collection are some of the distinct advantages.

ON DESK DUTY

Managing time at the Information Desk decrees certain ordinances. Staff the hectic hours with the least stress inclined librarians. Four hour blocks of time work well—no longer and shorter if necessary. Light activities only should be taken up and not plunged into which wards off students. Trying to complete a job requiring concentration often cheats student and librarian; stoking up more concentration after the abbreviated reference interview hinders clear thought. Since the desk is designed to be the hub of activity, the librarian should also be active. Standing and walking over to anticipate questions or to follow through on a reference lead saves time. Many students just do not warm to a busy-looking librarian, but do respond gratefully to one who crosses the floor to help. A student will wait for a formerly amicable librarian in lieu of approaching a curmudgeon again. When thorough assistance is given the first time, few return questions purloin minutes from the day. Activities difficult to essay at the Information Desk are: devising strategy for a computer search, compiling statistics for a report, or preparing a library manual. An activity more beneficial to IS would be to note brain teasers while visually inviting every inquiry.

The academic librarian knows that certain professors assign the same projects year after year. Thus, it is an unpardonable sin not to amass reference sources for the expected onslaught of students. Time management suffers if these sources are not earmarked or are missing. Just as recurring projects go to make the aware IS librarian's life easier, so too do recurring questions. Their answers should be rote memory and better sources sought for when the information is sketchy. Repertoire maintenance economizes on time. The IS librarian who is indecisive when faced with a chiming question causes lament.

The desire to locate the exact answer tempts many an IS librarian. Then the role of information counselor becomes that of fetcher. Over-servicing a student disallows initiative and the student learns but one lesson: find a fetcher librarian. There is a real art to leading a student to information without having to take the first drink. Other students compacted at the desk see the librarian lavishing time on a "new friend" and grow impatient. When to cut off the information interview to the mutual satisfaction of both parties has not been stored in a table. The one observation is that the more knowledgeable IS librarian deftly garners time while assisting a greater number of students, et al. For those who cannot turn their backs on an elusive answer, better time management would be to wait until off desk hours to go ferreting. The idea is to serve the many well, not just the few superbly. The coy answer found, the IS librarian with a penchant for enigmas will disclose the investigative steps at a meeting.

OFF DESK DUTY

The twenty hours worked at the Information Desk is verifiable time. But how to account for the other twenty which might be abused by inactivity? The purist can keep a log. The not so purist should at least write up a schedule as a gentle prod. Since any number of loose ends to knot occur everyday in IS, a strict schedule is impossible to adhere to. Some days information requests fly through the air like missiles and the *New York Times'* newsroom appears dead in comparison. The information riot has to be quelled and less vociferous pursuits put aside. Other days—nothing, and a schedule can be returned to. Flexibility is the key; pending work comes first, casual work second.

The schedule for off desk hours should embrace the staples of IS. Compiling bibliographies, collection development, liaison with teaching faculty, and weeding are such basic items. But also slated for attention should be reviewing books, conducting research, and brainstorming in general about IS and library operations. Depending on the needs of IS and personal preference, off desk hours might take this configuration:

Compilation of bibliographies*	3 hours
Collection development	3
Teaching faculty liaison*	3
Weeding*	2
Reviewing books	2
Conducting research	5
Brainstorming	2
	20 hours

Activities asterisked are not weekly endeavors unless they have been neglected for awhile. Substitutions can be made to include a host of other activities: committee work, mounting displays, student conferences, etc. The bibliographic instruction program might entail additional time for perfection. Sitting in on a computer course can be worthwhile for a novitiate to the Information Age. Do not think it fussy to type a prioritized schedule, otherwise hours will evaporate due to amorphism.

On a personal level, the IS librarian who emulates the scholar in a cell of yellowed, tumbling pages guillotines time searching for shards of work to complete. Spendthrift habits are piles of unanswered communications, stacks of books in the office which belong out on the shelves, mushrooming slips of paper with mental notes scribbled on them, and unweeded file cabinets. The cascade engulfs time management.

CONCLUSION

Time management relies on personal and administrative reorganization for its success. The person must adopt certain time honored work habits; administration must recognize the higher importance

IS can assume. Faculty status for academic librarians has been hard won. Now the challenge is to deserve the honor. Rife with clerical duties, IS can grind to a halt. Swelling with students one minute and deserted the next, staffing IS can mock accomplishment. The inclination is to subject staff to minor task completion and ready alert. Then the regret airs that time is unkind to those who wish to excel. In many ways the clock can be beaten as has been suggested. Also for consideration is to split the week into twenty hours on/off the Information Desk. To schedule ample free time for employments more in line with the teaching faculty is the object. No longer should IS staff act as infertile sentinels fronting the reference collection, when far reaching departmental performance can result from a simple restructuring of time.

REFERENCES

1. David W. Nicastro, "Tools & Techniques for Productive Management," *Security Management*, vol. 28, no. 4, April 1984, p. 47-49.
2. Warren Keith Schilit, "A Manager's Guide to Efficient Time Management," *Personnel Journal*, vol. 62, no. 9, September 1983, p. 736-742.
3. John P. Kotter, *The General Managers* (New York: The Free Press, 1982), p. 79-85.

Role of the Manager in Reference Staff Development

Margaret Hendley

Staff development is an integral part of human resource planning and management in any library. The needs and interests of the individual must be balanced against the needs and objectives of the organization. Crucial to maintaining this balance is the role of the department manager—the person with one foot in the general administration of the organization and the other firmly planted in the necessary details and closer focus of running a department.

I intend to examine this central role of the manager in reference staff development, specifically in the context of public libraries. After an introduction, including definition of terms, this paper will focus on five areas of concern: (1) necessity of working with established departmental and/or library policies, guidelines and budgets; (2) how to facilitate staff to work toward their individual goals and/or objectives, including decision making on the pursuit of the two avenues of development; (3) use of internal organizations and/or specialized staff for staff development; (4) use of external opportunities for staff development; and (5) how to plan for and facilitate your "graduates"—those who move up and out.

INTRODUCTION AND OVERVIEW

This vital role of the department manager is well expressed in the introduction of *Personnel Development in Libraries* where it is stated that "management strives to develop human resources to the satisfaction of both individual and organizational goals."[1] The balancing act this necessitates to do this effectively requires a sensitivity to individual needs as well as a firm understanding of and the

---

The author is Co-ordinator, Information Services, Kitchener Public Library, 85 Queen St. North, Kitchener, Ontario N2H 2H1.

© 1986 by The Haworth Press, Inc. All rights reserved.

ability to communicate the library and departmental goals and objectives.

Human resource planning is an area of extreme concern to all organizations today. Effective use of staff has been analyzed, probed and deliberated in hundreds of current publications—both in the business world and library profession. One of the more effective voices in this plethora of literature is James Walker, who divides human resource planning into three categories: (1) needs forecasting or improved planning and control over staffing and organizational requirements, based on analysis of conditions; (2) performance management, which involves improving the performance of individuals and of the organization as a whole; (3) career management which concerns activities to select, assign, develop and otherwise manage individual careers in an organization.[2] Staff development is not something done in isolation, or as icing on the cake of organizational goals. From the individual staff member's point of view, staff development might only seem a concern of the last area cited—career management. An effective manager, however, has been involved with needs forecasting and performance management long before reaching the specifics of determining and selecting from the variety of possible activities that can comprise "staff development".

DEFINITION OF TERMS

It is also essential to define staff development, as differentiated from either staff training or continuing education. Although there are elements common to all three activities there is a definite distinction of focus. Training activities are designed to provide employees with specific knowledge, skills and attitudes necessary to perform their responsibilities most effectively.[3] Staff development is broader in scope. It comprises a wide range of activities designed to provide staff with knowledge and skills related to their current (and possibly future) position in the organization. As well as teaching general skills, techniques and procedures staff development should include activities intended to provide employees with (a) understanding of organizational objectives and (b) general knowledge and concepts necessary to ensure effective performance.[4] Continuing education may encompass many of the same activities as staff development, but it has a different focus. It is a self-directed process, rather than an organizational directed one, which addresses the needs of the individual.[5]

What you hope to achieve with staff development depends of course upon your own particular working environment. Barbara Conroy, noted authority on library staff development, presents us with a comprehensive list of concerns: improve library efficiency, modify staff attitudes and/or boost staff morale, keep staff up-to-date, cope with any immediate or anticipated library problems and/or changes, build long range staff and library capacity.[6] Library staff development then, involves improving and developing the capabilities of individuals to achieve and maintain the highest possible quality of library service.

NEEDS ASSESSMENT

The role of the department manager in bringing about reference staff development is certainly a complex, but an extremely interesting and rewarding one. First, it is essential that one's "background work" be done. A needs assessment with established priorities is essential. The manager must examine the departmental structure and reporting mechanism, note any changing conditions in the library as a whole and weigh the informational needs of the community. Then, based on the knowledge of the strengths and weaknesses of individual staff members as well as departmental goals and objectives, he/she can begin to establish priorities for staff development. For example, staff turnover or promotions may necessitate some training in supervisory skills while a newly automated system could demand a more sophisticated computer background for all.

POLICIES AND BUDGETS

The manager must be firmly grounded in the knowledge of established library and departmental policies, guidelines and budgets in relation to human resource planning. For example, to know just how flexible time and money allotments allocated to the Reference Department for staff development in a given year would be essential information. This is not to say that a manger must take all traditional guidelines as written in stone. Presumably, reasonable access to the Chief Librarian and some participation in decision making on library policies puts the departmental manager in a position to recommend any changes in these policies (or exception to them), necessitated by particular circumstances. However, proper planning and anticipation of needs as previously outlined can avoid a slapdash approach to staff development.

COMMUNICATION TO STAFF

The communication of any library policies regarding staff development to all department members is another essential part of the role of the Reference Manager. Well defined policies and procedures which are made known to all the staff provide an environment in which individual staff can be encouraged to be active participants in determining their growth and development.[7] Clear cut guidelines regarding limitations on time and budget can prevent unrealistic expectations and eventual disappointments. For example, a library acting on the recommendations of the Reference Manager might provide release time (and/or money) for a subject specialist to take a short course in a related area at a nearby university, but might not provide either time or money for another staff member working toward a Bachelors or Masters degree in an area unrelated to his/her work.

FUNDING FOR STAFF DEVELOPMENT

Knowledge of the existing budget for staff development and the possibility of tapable sources outside the library is also vital. Frequently the library's Personnel Director will centralize this information so that various department managers have easy access to it. Many libraries are supported in their human resource development by available funding from the state or province. For instance, in the state of Maryland, public libraries may apply for staff development mini-grants to help defray costs for any in-service training. In addition, public librarians, acting through their employers, may request up to two thirds reimbursement grants to help defray costs of attending workshops and academic courses.[8] In Ontario, the Ministry of Citizenship and Culture, which is responsible for public libraries, has recently announced that Wintario Grants are to be made available for skills training and staff development in public libraries. Priority will be given to staff development in the areas of management and technical skills pertinent to automation.[9] The well-informed Reference Manager would investigate and take into account all possible funding options when planning departmental staff development, particularly if any sort of major outlay of funds would be involved. Ignorance of such funding sources (and any directions or limitations attached to them) can make the difference between a positive or negative reception on the part of administration to your recommendations.

Therefore, in planning for any reference staff development the department manager should (a) establish priorities based upon needs assessment; (b) be thoroughly familiar with any library policies and budgets which would affect human resource planning; and (c) communicate these policies to all departmental staff members. In addition, in any library that is unionized, the manager should have all the necessary specifics on how union regulations do or do not affect such areas as job assignments, working hours, etc., which again, could influence planning for staff development.

JOB ENVIRONMENT

With this background work done, how can the Reference Manager proceed with professional development in the department? First, would be a strong awareness that both well defined formal as well as informal means play a role. The latter concerns the general environment in the work place. The departmental manager is largely responsible for setting the tone—hopefully creating a climate conducive to growth. Many consider the employee's supervisor as the most important influence affecting staff development and growth.[10] Attitudes are hard to spell out but are definitely pervasive. Staff are quick to know—and to communicate to newcomers—if the departmental manager is open to opportunities for all staff to grow and develop professionally, whatever their status within the department. Open communication and flexible attitudes toward new ideas all contribute to this overall atmosphere.

MOTIVATION OF STAFF

Perhaps one of the strongest factors in creating this environment is the ability—or lack of it—for the Reference Manager to motivate his/her staff to continually stretch to reach their highest capacity. While the base line for any individual is ultimately self-motivation, the effective Reference Manager can go a long way toward producing desired results by careful observation of, effective communication with, concern for and sensitivity to the needs, problems and aspirations of each staff person for which he/she is responsible.[11] Only then is he/she in any kind of a position to recommend staff development for specific individuals.

Perhaps less idealistically, Conroy spells out some specific incentives that can be used to motivate staff involvement in their development. They range from a "high" of esteem and praise to a "low" of penalties for nonparticipation with such suggestions in between as: credit in performance appraisal, salary or merit increases, opportunities for promotion and reassignment, documentation of participation in the personnel file and special privileges.[12] Certainly a number of these are worthy of consideration and the wise Reference Manager should at least be aware of their possibility.

INDIVIDUALITY OF STAFF

Essential throughout, however, is the recognition that staff development is based on maximizing the capabilities of individuals. It is specific with recognition of the uniqueness of each person within a department.[13] Staff must be studied, both in the formal atmosphere of job evaluations which will be dealt with at a later point, as well as in the informal, on-going basis of day-to-day performance. Key individuals whose contributions are considered essential to meeting objectives in the area where they work must be identified.[14]

Strengths and weaknesses in relation to departmental current and future needs should be noted to determine recommended development programs.

The crunch can come at the next stage—working together with individuals to be aware of their options within a particular library and departmental structure and possibly influencing the direction in which they choose to move, dependent always upon the needs of the organization.

TWO "STREAMS" OF DEVELOPMENT: SUBJECT SPECIALIZATION AND SUPERVISORY/MANAGEMENT

Few Reference Managers, anyway, would disagree with the statement that this function of differentiation is an extremely complicated one in reference and information services. Usually opportunities abound for a variety of subject specializations and the depth to which they can be pursued are limited only by the eternal restraints of time and money. Yet reference staff are also in dire need of good managers. Assuming some kind of limitations on funds, and the fact that the staff development "pie" must be shared with other departments, how do you determine between recommendations for development in subject specializations and management/supervisory skills? In many cases, by doing some kind of "juggle" but hopefully an educated one based upon the background work and identification of individual needs and aspirations discussed earlier. Certainly communication to the Administration of what you see as the particular problems of choosing among the diversity of training and development options peculiar to the Reference Department can't hurt—as long as you refrain from sounding like a broken record, indifferent to the library needs as a whole.

OPPORTUNITIES FOR STAFF DEVELOPMENT INTERNAL TO THE SYSTEM

There are innumerable activities for a Reference Manager to consider for staff development opportunities within the organization. This, perhaps, is the "plus" side of the complexity of needs and interests in Reference Departments. Within the department itself flexibility in regard to the assignment of special projects outside the normal scheduled desk time and routine responsibilities is a real plus. For the less experienced or nonprofessional staff the chance to produce a resource list, prepare and deliver a user education presentation to a visiting group, or participate in a mall display can be a real opportunity for growth and development. Obviously the manager here must take into account any need for guidance and training as well as work within whatever limitations that detailed job descriptions (and/or union regulations) impose. Also, the completion of any such special work assignments and the person's interest—or lack of it—in these areas should be noted and recorded.

INVOLVEMENT IN COMMITTEES

One of the most effective tools for staff development within the organization is the opportunity for individuals to work on departmental and/or library committees. There are three general types of committees: first, Standing Committees, which are ongoing and frequently have appointed members; second, Annual Committees, which have a specific job to do each year and are then disbanded; and third, Special Committees, which are viable as long as necessary to deal with special projects or current pressing issues.[15]

Whether ongoing or struck for a particular task, such committees offer the opportunity for growth and development to all of its members. On an interdepartmental committee an individual has the opportunity to not only represent his/her department's point of view, but hear first hand the attitudes and ideas of others working in different sections of the library. Whether elected, appointed or a volunteer, the individual is presented with a broader base of experience than ordinary in his/her work and the option to work with others to solve a mutual problem.

PARTICIPATORY MANAGEMENT

An intradepartmental committee offers the option for participatory management. This is considered by many to be one of the best ways to develop the skills needed for future leadership in the library. Its major strength is the involvement of the staff in the decision making process. Through such a committee staff are taught to pay attention to the realities of organizational fact related to the specific matter at hand. Leadership qualities that are developed through such interaction include the capacity to mediate, the ability to plan and the power to analyze feedback.[16] Participatory management also can provide the individual with evaluation of his competence in an (hopefully) unthreatening environment. Ideally, in a supportive atmosphere an intradepartmental committee can result in the development of peer group loyalty, improved coordination and effective interaction.[17]

Two "negatives" should be noted, however. One, decision making by participatory management is slower than by individual leadership; and two, in most public libraries, it is extremely difficult to wangle enough time to meet with the whole Reference Department on a regular basis sufficient to make all decisions. The service to the public must go on and if the hours staff work largely coincide with the hours the library is "open to business" someone must mind the store! It is important at any rate for the Reference Manager to take into account the strong role participatory management can play in staff development and consider integrating such a process into the department as much as possible.

LIBRARY WORKSHOPS

Staff meetings and library workshops can also provide the opportunity for growth and development. Depending on departmental needs and specialization available within the system some or all of the department can be asked to participate in a program intended to provide increased knowledge or ability to deal with a particular type of subject area. For example, a session might be devoted to the discussion of government publications and how they can be utilized to answer business questions. If a specialist within the department leads the workshop, that person also benefits by gaining experience in planning and presenting a program to a particular group.

JOB ROTATION

Another option to consider with strong developmental possibilities is job rotation within the system. Today's economic conditions might prevent as much opportunity for external courses, workshops, etc. as the Reference Manager considers ideal. A chance to experience first-hand another function in the library for a period of time could be a valuable addition to someone's vita as well as provide enrichment to the departments concerned. For example, a person newly hired or promoted as an Assistant in a Branch could find it valuable to have the in-depth reference experience found working for a period in the Reference Department of the central library. In exchange, a staff member from reference would work in the Branch gaining supervisory experience perhaps not available within the department. Obviously much planning and careful training would be necessary on both sides. Also, the type of sensitivity to individuals and identification of their strengths and weaknesses that were discussed earlier as a function of the Reference Manager would be vital here to select the right staff person with leadership ability to benefit from such a job rotation.

EXTERNAL OPPORTUNITIES

Participation in conferences, workshops and seminars external to the particular library system are what come to mind to most people when thinking of staff development. Indeed their contribution is invaluable and the usual problem for the Reference Manager is selection—which programs would best suit the identified needs of the department (and library) and which staff should be selected to participate. The usual time/money factors discussed earlier and selection process again play a strong part in the decision making. Frequently information on upcoming programs whether from library associations, graduate library schools or other sources are centralized in the system so that all department managers have access to it. Asking the staff member to provide feedback to the department, such as making a report at a department meeting or initiating some special project based on information gained from a workshop also constitute part of the skills development of attending a conference or workshop.

PARTICIPATION IN COMMITTEES EXTERNAL TO SYSTEM

Participating as a member of a professional or job related committee, whether on the national, state/provincial, regional or local level, can be an extremely valuable experience. Professional organizations are often looking for eager workers and active new members. Participation could involve such activities as sitting on a Standing Committee, working on preparing a brief or report, or planning and/or participating in a workshop for a future conference—all definitely learning activities as anyone who has convened a workshop will attest! A manager who encourages staff to consider this sort of involvement is opening yet another avenue of development.

On the local level there are even more possibilities. Public libraries in particular are community oriented and close links with certain special interest community associations can be useful for both organizations. A Reference Department, for example, might find it mutually beneficial to have the Business Librarian participate in certain Chamber of Commerce meetings and activities. Obviously, one must be very selective if library time is involved—all interests can not and should not be considered as "professional" activities. Job relatedness and clearly defined priorities based on departmental objectives are the key to judging—and communicating—to the staff just what might constitute an officially sanctioned "liaison" function between library and organization and what must be deemed a private interest.

Participation in such groups, whether local or on a broader scale, reaps the same benefits as discussed earlier with internal library committees, with the added strength that in this instance one is often representing the whole library which can give added weight—and responsibility—to a single voice. Again, follow-through on any such activities should include regular reporting to the Reference Manager and notation by the manager in the liaison person's file so that a current record is available of all professional activities.

JOB EXCHANGE

Job exchange with another librarian—possibly even in another country—is an adventuresome developmental option that might have great appeal to some on staff. This topic is dealt with in detail in the book, *Staff Exchanges in Librarianship* where it is recommended that such exchanges are best suited between specific areas of specialization.[18] Such an experience would have many possibilities for staff development, but the administrative details to arrange such a program would be onerous to many managers.

PLANNING FOR YOUR "GRADUATES"

Having contemplated all the options of staff development discussed previously and put the best suited into action, how then does the Reference Manager plan for and facilitate the "graduates"—those who move up and out of their original position—and possibly the department? In some cases, perhaps, merely with a congratulatory smile and a handshake. In others, however, a good deal more is expected.

In many cases, the development or career path of an individual has been a gradual process involving identification by the manager, communication with the staff person and specific action. A manager can make at least a mental note when someone seems ripe for change and plan accordingly so that gaping holes can be avoided. "Back-up," or certain staff having the flexibility to work at least temporarily in a variety of areas essential to the ongoing functioning of the department, can be extremely helpful in a variety of situations, including dealing with any sudden departures.

In some instances, an area of specialization within the department may grow to the extent that it is decided by Administration to establish a separate department. Such changes are usually felt gradually, with growing demand by the public for more in-depth services, often paralleling the development of a staff member in a subject area, such as local history. It is crucial in the planning and transition period that open communication between Administration and concerned staff be maintained. Questions about resources, staffing and service should be discussed thoroughly and clear decisions made so that the implementation of service to the public in a new department be as smooth as possible.

PERFORMANCE APPRAISAL

Another process which can play a strong role in planning for staff development is the Performance Appraisal. Many systems have a specific spot on the appraisal or evaluation form for the manager's comments regarding any need for or interest in some area of an individual's development. Certainly it is an opportunity for the manager to discuss any future aspirations with the staff member and help him/her to set specific learning objectives.[19] Depending upon the structure of the particular library system a referral to the Personnel Director might be recommended—for example, to discuss options for supervisory experience within the library system. The manager can help the individual to review the year's work, not only in relation to performance, but also in relation to what provided the most job satisfaction to the individual. This information, paralleled by the manager's knowledge of the various career opportunities in the library, can facilitate a realistic plan of development objectives. This plan should make clear what might be possible through the library staff development program and what should be undertaken as an individually motivated continuing education endeavor. In the Performance Appraisal interview open communication concerning an individual's future plans would certainly be enhanced if the manager has established the atmosphere discussed earlier where staff are aware that growth and development are encouraged.

CONCLUSION

Because one must deal sensitively with individual needs and aspirations at the same time as working toward departmental goals and objectives, the function of human resource planning and management is an extremely complex one. Done successfully, however, staff development can be one of the most rewarding responsibilities of the Reference Manager.

REFERENCES

1. *Personnel Development in Libraries. Proceedings of the Thirteenth Annual Symposium sponsored by the Alumni and the Faculty of the Rutgers University Graduate School of Library Science*, ed. by R. Kay Maloney (New Brunswick, New Jersey: Rutgers University, 1976), p. ix.
2. James Walker, *Human Resource Planning* (New York: McGraw-Hill, 1980), p. 10.
3. *Personnel Administration in Libraries*, ed. by Shelia Creth and Frederick Duda (New York: Neal-Schuman Pub., 1981), p. 197.
4. Ibid., p. 190.
5. Ibid., p. 217.
6. Barbara Conroy, *Library Staff Development Profile Pages. A Guide and Workbook for Library Self Assessment and Planning* (Granby, Colorado: Country Printer, 1979), p. 14.
7. *Personnel Administration*, p. 220.
8. Sandy Stephan, "Continuing Education in Maryland," *Public Libraries*, Spring 1984, p. 26.
9. Statement from application form for Wintario Grants from the Ontario Ministry of Citizenship and Culture, 1984.
10. "Guidelines to the Development of Human Resources in Libraries: Rationale, Policies, Programs and Recommendations," *Library Trends*, July 1971, p. 107.
11. Charles Goodman, "Incentives and Motivation for Staff Development," *New Directions in Staff Development. Moving from Ideas to Action*, ed. by Elizabeth Stone (Chicago: American Library Association, 1971), pp. 56-57.
12. Conroy, p. 11.
13. Robert and Charlene Lee, "Personnel Planning for a Library Manpower System," *Library Trends*, July 1971, p. 34.
14. Ibid., p. 26.
15. Grace P. Slocum, "Participation by Committee," *New Directions in Staff Development. Moving from Ideas to Actions*, ed. by Elizabeth Stone (Chicago: American Library Association, 1971), p. 49.
16. Maurice Marchant, "Participative Management as Related to Personnel Development," *Library Trends*, July 1971, p. 57.
17. Lee, p. 30.
18. Susunaga Weeraperuma, *Staff Exchanges in Librarianship* (London: Poets' and Painters' Press, 1970), p. 39.
19. Patricia King, *Performance Planning and Appraisal. A How-To Book for Managers* (New York: McGraw-Hill, 1984), pp. 15-16.

Quality Control of Reference Service in Branch Libraries of a Multi-Campus College

Pamela L. Wonsek

A typical reference department is made up of professionals who interact daily, share common experiences in serving common clients, and share a common reference collection. In Mercy College Libraries' Branch and External Services Division the challenge is to maintain uniform quality standards of library service and library instruction throughout a "reference department" made up of four geographically separated libraries, with each librarian serving a different population. In training, motivating, supervising, and evaluating professionals in such a department, the manager must utilize the benefits of centralization while fostering the enthusiasm and creativity that can be generated from this diversity. Management of such a unit also presents special challenges in ensuring that each library and librarian is committed to the same principles and standards of service and is performing at the same high quality level. An essential component to such management must be an effective formal and informal feedback system which allows for continual communication to flow in both directions.

In order to manage a group of separate libraries which are designed to function as parts of one system there must exist a common thread which binds all libraries together. There must be a common understanding of mutual goals and standards for excellence. In his *Management: Tasks, Responsibilities, Practices*, Peter Drucker outlined six components necessary to manage a service institution for performance: (1) definition of purpose; (2) clear objectives and goals; (3) priorities of concentration; (4) measurement of per-

---

Ms. Wonsek is Head of Branch and External Services at Mercy College Libraries, Dobbs Ferry, NY (Westchester County). She supervises the four branch and extension libraries located at the Yorktown Heights Branch Campus and White Plains, Yonkers, and the Bronx Centers.

© 1986 by The Haworth Press, Inc. All rights reserved.

formance; (5) feedback on efforts; and (6) organized audit of objectives and results.[1] With this framework in place the branch librarian can identify his or her role and determine how that role functions within the system.

ESTABLISHING THE GOALS

Although the purpose of the academic branch library is identical to the mission of a branch public library, i.e., "to give as much and as good service to as many citizens in its area as possible,"[2] academic branch libraries functioning as a system must also be tied to the overall system's mission and goals. The library system's mission and goals must be compatible with the academic institution's mission statement. The establishment of such goals for the system as well as the branches allows for the determination of what is defined as quality service. In a library system that sees its role as central to the academic experience at all locations and is dedicated to aggressive and proactive outreach efforts, this definition of quality service must be thoroughly understood. It goes beyond the excellence of the collection and the reference service but also is measured by the vitality of the sales promotion activity. Once the commitment is given to the standards, and goals are established, a systematic process of determining the objectives to be used in reaching these goals begins. The development of specific department and personal objectives with quantifiable outcomes is linked carefully to goals and mission statements of branch library, library system and ultimately the institution itself. The participation of the branch librarians in the development of all of the above serves to focus their awareness of the role they play, the standards they must attain, and provides a workable framework for supervision, performance appraisals and staff development. This is the crucial foundation which allows the branch librarians to function in a semi-autonomous fashion while ensuring that their actions are directly related to the overall direction of the library system.

CENTRALIZATION AND UNIFORMITY

As the library system concept has been developing at Mercy College over a period of eight years, decisions on the appropriate centralization versus decentralization of functions, personnel and services have been established, modified, strengthened and systemized. Some decisions are clear-cut. Since each branch library was conceived as a public service unit, all technical operations are centralized for economic and space efficiency. But what happens to public service functions, especially reference service and library instruction? Do they lend themselves to centralization? From the vantage point of a manager who must monitor the quality of service provided at remote locations, the centralization within the system of all policies, procedures and standards is essential. However, as underlined in *Wheeler and Goldhor's Practical Administration of Public Libraries*, "uniformity should not be sought for its own sake but only for other results clearly to be gained and more desirable than the results of decentralization." One can see that with multiple library locations at campuses within easy traveling distance of each other it would be folly to have library policies anything other than uniform. Students and faculty using more than one center during a given semester, year or even college career should not be expected to reorient themselves to different levels of library service. For example, when library instruction is given for a course at one location a faculty member must be assured that the library instruction is given in a similar fashion, and with the same quality, when the course is offered at a different location. Without the uniformity of reference service and library instruction at all locations it would be impossible for the manager to judge the quality of services delivered.

DECENTRALIZATION AND AUTONOMY

With these standards in place each branch librarian must capitalize on the decentralization and autonomy that occurs naturally. In all areas where uniformity and centralization are not crucial to the effective delivery of library services, each branch librarian must function as an individual entrepreneur. This autonomy can be used as a motivating factor by the manager to encourage creative and innovative ideas to promote library services. An example of this would be promotional efforts. Techniques and strategies used at the Central Campus would not be adequate or appropriate to the dynamics of any of the branch campuses. The branch librarian must use his or her autonomy to mobilize whatever efforts are necessary to meet the needs of the unique clientele of each branch location. In this role the branch librarian must become the specialist in knowing exactly which needs are to be met and the most successful strategies to implement. The performance of the branch librarian can then be measured by the manager in terms of outcome results. This individual entrepreneurship must be encouraged by the manager not only because of its results but also for its rejuvenative effect on the entire library system. The advantage of individual experimentation is that results can be fed back into the system and contribute to a dynamic and non-static philosophy of library service. Often ideas initiated at one location, when reported, are modified and used in another location.

MBO IN PLANNING AND CONTROL

Certainly it is not enough merely to establish quality standards; a structure must exist within the system that allows for continual monitoring of the service levels. Is the library instruction program meeting the needs of all potential users? Are the library lectures of uniform quality? Is the book collection being developed in a systematic fashion that relates directly to the curriculum of the branch campus? Clearly, formal controls are required in order to monitor these and other activities at separate campuses.

Management by objectives is the planning system that the Mercy College Libraries employ which also functions as a control mechanism to assist the manager in monitoring the performance levels of the staff. Once a year each librarian develops a set of individual department and personal objectives which will be undertaken throughout the coming year. These objectives are measurable and require specific actions to be taken within a designated time period by the individual librarian responsible for their accomplishment. Each branch librarian develops several different objectives within each area of his or her responsibility, resulting in a strategic planning document which shows how and when activities will be undertaken at the branch library. In consultation with the manager these objectives are modified, some added, and some dropped until the document is acceptable to librarian, manager, and top administration.

The critiquing of the proposed objectives by the manager is of vital importance since it will set the tone for the remainder of the year. Although the manager cannot formulate the objectives for the librarian it would be counterproductive to approve a set of objectives that are not challenging, do not move the library service ahead, do not reflect the primary public service functions of the branch, or are not in line with the overall system goals for library service. The manner in which each branch librarian develops new objectives is a clear indicator to the manager of how the librarian sees the branch library developing over the next year and how he or she is expecting to perform. If a librarian is not committed to the same quality standards as the library system, this often becomes apparent during the objectives' writing phase.

ACCOUNTABILITY AND PERFORMANCE APPRAISAL

The reporting of the accomplishment of the objectives is another important control mechanism. Since the objectives as written include target completion dates, each librarian monitors his or her own performance by reporting progress in a required monthly report. This forced accountability in a consistent, timely fashion ensures that once written, these objectives are not filed away. In January, mid-point of the academic year, the manager meets with each librarian to review the progress of all the objectives. This step supplements the monthly reports as a means of providing feedback on performance in a structured fashion, allowing sufficient time for needed change and modification before the formal performance appraisal.

Stueart and Eastlick suggest that standards of performance against which employees can be measured fall into three categories: quality-quantity standards, desired effect standards, and manner of performance standards.[4] In evaluating the performance of the branch librarians the manager must make use of the entire objectives process in order to make meaningful appraisals within Stueart and Eastlick's first two categories. It is not sufficient, however, only to judge the accomplishment of the objective; the manner in which the objectives were developed and how closely they reflected the system's goals are at least as important to the manager. In his article, "Appraisal of *what* performance," psychologist Harry Levinson cautions managers from relying exclusively on the outcome of behavior without sufficient regard for the behavior itself[5]—Stueart and Eastlick's third category.

CRITICAL INCIDENT PROCESS

The separateness of the branch libraries and the formal reporting structure lends itself more readily to the evaluation of outcomes alone. A deliberate effort must be made by the manager to gather meaningful objective data within highly subjective areas of behavior and interpersonal interaction. How flexible is the librarian; how open to new ideas; how creative at solving problems; how responsive to criticism; how open to constant feedback and communication? One approach that can be useful in documenting such subjective areas is the critical incident process. Long discussed and used within business,[6] this technique has been adapted to library management as well.[7] Levinson defines the critical incident process in this way:

> So that there will be useful data, the manager needs to quickly write down what he has said to the subordinate, describing in a paragraph what the subordinate did or did not do, in what setting, under what circumstances, about what problem. This information forms a *behavioral* record, a critical incident report of which the subordinate already has been informed and which is now in his folder, open to his review . . . one might directly record the behavior of those being appraised, and evaluate it at a later date . . . At last, here is a process that provides data to help managers perform the basic functions of performance appraisal systems—namely provide feedback, coaching, and promotion data.[8]

Without such a written record of formal and informal contacts, positive and negative behavior, it would be impossible to construct a meaningful assessment of an entire year's performance. Keeping in mind that performance evaluation can serve an important staff development function, it is as essential that the manager be able to document how the librarian fell short of satisfying the system's quality standards in both behavior and outcomes as it is to reinforce the truly outstanding behavior and outcomes. Shortcomings then must become areas of special development and emphasis as the objectives are planned for the next year. In this manner performance evaluation works hand-in-hand with the objectives process in the assurance and maintenance of quality library standards.

HIRING NEW STAFF

The responsibility for acclimating new staff to the library system rests with the manager of branch libraries as it does with the manager of a reference department. One difference in this process may be found in the intensity of the initial orientation period which *must* prepare the branch librarian to operate solo in the shortest possible time. The personal characteristics of the person hired are probably the most significant indicators of the librarian's future success in a branch position. Since major job functions of the branch librarian are assertive outreach, public relations, library instruction and reference, a librarian is sought who is not only self-motivated, energetic and outgoing but also is committed to the same philosophical goals as the library system. Not all academic librarians see themselves in such a proactive role; while they may be effective spokespersons for library service, they are not necessarily comfortable as salespersons. Perhaps such an individual could be coached, guided, or motivated to develop such attitudes within many traditional settings by receiving daily observation and feedback; this daily contact is not possible at a branch and consequently the wrong person in the wrong job quickly could become demoralized and not be effective. Therefore, in selection of a new librarian, "entrepreneur" characteristics must be apparent and are more desirable than specific job skills such as selection or knowledge of audio-visual equipment—these can be taught on the job.

TRAINING NEW STAFF

It would be a disservice to any new librarian, regardless of talent, to send him or her out alone with only policy manual in hand and expect him or her to make the branch library work. Only with a solid foundation in how the Central Library and the system work can the new librarian begin to understand his or her role. All new branch librarians receive an extensive orientation at the Central Library, working long hours at the reference desk to develop their awareness of the full level of support (materials, personnel, and services) available to them through the Central Library. Following this period, which includes a thorough review of all policy and procedure manuals, the new librarian works briefly at one or two branch libraries to observe the similarities and differences of each location.

These steps are essential in building a staff that operates as a team and is fully cognizant of its role within the library system. Only then does the librarian take charge of the branch library.

While effective two-way communication between manager and librarian is always important, it is most crucial during these weeks of orientation. Patterns of communication and feedback established during this period can easily determine the success of the relationship in the future. Initially daily meetings are scheduled to review questions, problems, or even to once again discuss the philosophical issues raised during the interview—connotations of which may not have been completely understood. Once the new librarian has left the Central Library it is useful to establish a definite time each day to at least speak by telephone. Such contact reinforces the link that ties librarian to manager, confirming once again that the librarian, although working alone, is supported by and accountable to a well-defined and structured system.

Although valuable, the initial training at the Central Library and review of policy and procedure manuals still remain somewhat out of context until work at the branch library has begun. Reinforcing the initial training can be accomplished by bringing the librarian back to the Central Library about once a week for a couple of months to work again at the reference desk and spend time with other library departments. This scheduling affords the librarian the flexibility of storing questions that do not need immediate answers and investigating solutions on one's own at a separate time. During this period, the manager blocks out a two-hour conference period on a weekly basis to thoroughly review problems, questions and dilemmas. This phase of training is most tempting to short-cut in light of staffing shortages at the branches. Limiting this phase, however, is trading a short-term gain for long-term problems.

DEVELOPING INDEPENDENCE AND AUTONOMY

Weaning the new librarian from total reliance on the manager and Central Library to provide direction in all decisions and encouraging the librarian to independence now becomes essential. How soon this happens depends upon the experience of the librarian and the desire for autonomy. The manager must deliberately refrain from providing the easy answer and must instead begin to ask how the librarian would handle the solution. The manner in which the new branch librarian defines the problem, evaluates the options, and proposes solutions reflecting a grasp of library policy and service philosophy is the mark of his or her development. Caution must be taken with a new librarian who quickly can propose solutions on the surface of which appear correct, however. The manger must probe the thought process to ensure that decisions are based on appropriate criteria.

This training and development phase often is as beneficial to the manager as it is for the new librarian. If high-powered and creative people are hired, they can bring new insights and solutions to problems. Just because the proposed decision is not one that would have occurred to the manager should not be grounds alone for dismissing it. Fostering and supporting independent and creative decision-making on the part of the new librarian must become a high priority for the manager. To do otherwise can lead to the development of a team tied to the Central Library with a strangulating umbilical cord. The branch librarians might never do anything wrong but they also will not do much that is innovative, exciting or requires risk.

COMMUNICATION AND FEEDBACK

Once the initial training phase has been completed the manager and librarian move into a "keep me informed of what is important" stage. Since the manager can never observe all daily routines firsthand, a mechanism to ensure timely and productive feedback on a continual basis is necessary. The branch librarian must keep the manager aware of what is happening by telephone or memorandum; the manager routinely must schedule on-site visits, both expected and unexpected, to observe exactly how the branch is functioning.

Formal monthly reports are not only excellent communication tools but they also serve as a self-monitoring device for the librarian's performance. These narrative monthly reports, to which pertinent public service statistics are appended, have evolved at Mercy College Libraries from brief cover memoranda to statistical sheets into their present structured form. The format of these reports requires the branch librarian to report on all areas of responsibility—Public Services, Reference, Library Instruction, Collection Development, Audio-Visual Services, Facilities, and Objectives. This reporting process forces each librarian to describe the monthly events in meaningful terms: What activities furthered the goals of the library; has an unexpected pattern of library use begun to emerge; what success did the library have in reaching new users; which objectives were completed; what effect did the objectives have on service?

Essentially the monthly reports become the manager's and top administrator's window into the branch library. Receiving such insights into how the branch is functioning provides necessary information to the manager to allow immediate follow-up and feedback by telephone or meeting. With such a formal reporting structure there is the opportunity to address potential performance problems early, rather than wait until a year-end review. By the same token, since these reports also allow the librarian to document accomplishments, the manager must respond with timely positive feedback and reward outstanding efforts just as quickly as criticism is given. Unless positive reinforcement is given in sufficient quantity for approved behavior, morale could suffer under the weight of a system which pressures and challenges its entire staff constantly to produce more and better results.

BUILDING AN EFFECTIVE BRANCH TEAM

Thus far the discussion has centered on the one-to-one interaction between manager and branch librarian. Evolving out of the commonality of experience, the branch librarians must function as a team—much as an effective reference department does. Without working elbow-to-elbow each day, the branch librarians must share common experiences, transfer information, support each other, and learn from each other. This esprit-de-corps is established early by including the branch librarians in the training schedule of a new branch librarian. Branch librarians can and should be sounding boards for each other as new ideas are being developed and as solutions to problems are being sought. Although there is no opportunity informally to meet during a coffee break, the telephone serves as a vital life-line. This spirit of comradeship must be encouraged by the manager since it serves not only to combat isolation but also results in healthy competition as branch librarians challenge, motivate and rejuvenate each other.

The development of such a team also requires a formal structure as well. Monthly branch meetings are scheduled to discuss administrative issues, share ideas, and resolve problems as a group. These monthly meetings rotate to all libraries including the Central Library, once again supporting the principle of a system of libraries and a team of librarians all dedicated to the same mutual goals, while at the same time giving the librarians a chance to appreciate the uniqueness of each location.

OBSERVING THE LIBRARY SERVICE

On-site evaluation and inspection is the ultimate tool that the manager must use to ensure the maintenance of quality service at all branch libraries. Assurance must be given to the manager and top administration that the written and verbal communication is in fact a true and accurate picture of what is happening at the branch library. This evaluation is accomplished in the following manner: reviewing the reference question log-book and discussing the types of questions and how they were answered; the formal observation of one or more library instruction classes per year to determine their success and quality; observing the use pattern, activity and vitality at different times of the day and evening during unannounced visits. None of the above are new or revolutionary ideas to the reference manager; however, they perhaps are more easily implemented when contact and observation can be maintained every day over an extended period of time. With supervision of branch libraries the on-site picture alone becomes somewhat impressionistic and could be taken out of context unless supported by the elaborate and structured system of communication and feedback as outlined above.

Finally, it must be foremost in the manager's goals to build a branch library team that is based on trust and mutual support. Since the manager cannot be at all locations at all times, the manager must have confidence that the team is functioning at the same high quality level. Of critical importance with this system is the explicit understanding that the burden of building such confidence lies with the branch librarians themselves. By the same token, the branch librarians must have confidence that the manager will apply quality standards uniformly and not whimsically, confidence that the manager will support their efforts, and confidence that rewards will be forthcoming for outstanding performance. Within such a high-powered, values-driven, and performance-oriented system there can be no tolerance for the non-performer. However, personal and professional rewards can be great for the high-energy, self-motivated individual who thrives on pressure and challenge.

REFERENCES

1. Peter F. Drucker, *Management: Tasks, Responsibilities, Practices* (New York: Harper & Row, 1974), p. 158-159.
2. *Wheeler and Goldhor's Practical Administration of Public Libraries*, Rev. ed. (New York: Harper & Row, 1981), p. 150.
3. Ibid., p. 249.
4. Robert D. Stueart and John Taylor Eastlick, *Library Management* (Littleton, Colo.: Libraries Unlimited, 1977), p. 101.
5. Harry Levinson, "Appraisal of *What* Performance?" *Harvard Business Review* 54 (July-August 1976): 30-36.
6. Ibid., p. 34.
7. Dimity S. Berkner, "Library Staff Development Through Performance Appraisal," *College & Research Libraries* 40 (July 1979): 335-344.
8. Levinson, "Appraisal of *What* Performance?" pp. 34-36.

PREPARATION FOR THE JOB, RECRUITMENT, CONTINUING EDUCATION AND OTHER CONCERNS

Everybody Needs Information

Miles M. Jackson

The extent to which an individual has the ability to gain access to information often determines the degree to which that individual will be personally effective in today's world. The people who use information appreciate its power to change things. On a very simple level without adequate information an individual cannot effectively correct wrongs, solve personal problems or make sound decisions. This is especially true in today's "information society."

Over the past decade persistent questions beg to be answered, especially in behavioral terms: How and where do people get *all* of their information? How much do we know about human internal factors that drive information seeking?

Libraries are only one part of the many systems in the information environment that are dedicated to providing information. Paramount to designing information delivery systems is the recognition that all people need information, despite their demographic characteristics. Decision making is not limited to corporate cultures where more and more employees have access to information and information processing tools. Research has been able to ascertain that on a personal level information can help individuals understand their life situation and decrease uncertainty. However, there are people who are informationally deprived and are often the segment of the population which tends to lack survival information related to satisfying basic human needs.

Despite the huge sums of money spent through federal programs citizens continue lacking adequate information to meet their needs. Research has only begun to tap the surface of the problem. As an example information seeking is now recognized as multi dimensional and can only be fully understood through our knowledge of such fields as behavioral sciences, economics and political science. The knowledge we have about information seeking as a human social

---

The author is Dean, Graduate School of Library Studies, University of Hawaii at Manoa, 2550 The Mall, Honolulu, Hawaii, 96822.

strategy is primarily based on two research traditions from communication and information studies: (1) information diffusion and (2) information needs.

INFORMATION DIFFUSION

Earlier studies in information diffusion suggested that information often flows from the mass media to individuals who were identified as opinion leaders and from these to less active sections in the population. Paul F. Lazarsfeld, Bernard Berelson, Elihu Katz and Everett Rogers were among the leaders in the late 1940's and 1950's who pioneered in tracing the patterns of information diffusion. The results of their research proved the basis for the "two-step flow" theory of communication. These studies found that people are strongly influenced by "other" types of individuals and in many cases more so than by mass media. The hypothesis holds that communication from the mass media to the general public is mediated by opinion leaders. Prior to the "two-step flow" hypotheses of information diffusion it was felt that users of print and broadcast media were a mass of disconnected individuals who were linked in some way to the media. The two-step flow theory when offered was a unique approach to understanding more about the dynamics of interpersonal communication information flow and the use of mass media. Although the theory is controversial among some communication experts, it still is one widely accepted approach to information flow. Despite the pervasiveness of the broadcast media, especially television, most individuals use interpersonal communication channels causing people to be strong intervening variables in information transfer. Another key variable in the diffusion process is the opinion leader.

Contrary to what many people think opinion leaders need not occupy positions of leadership i.e., political office holder, teacher, preacher nor any type of elite. In fact, their chief characteristics might well be that they have no specific demographic characteristics such as race, age, sex, occupation or income. They can be everyday people we have all known in school, organizations or on the job. Opinion leaders as information carriers are simply people who consciously or unconsciously influence the opinions and attitudes of others by serving as information sources. They are likely to be heavy library users but also are likely to get their information through a variety of media and channels—broadcast, print and person to person.

INFORMATION NEEDS

The ability of librarians to fully understand information seeking behavior requires comprehension of the nature of information needs. In general, studies of information needs have often been related to library user studies. User studies were primarily for planning information services for libraries and most frequently focused on people who were already using the library and belonged to mostly professional or scientific groups. Further, research focus on the information needs of professionals and scientific researchers managed to persist to the neglect of the informationally deprived. Perhaps the lag in pursuing information needs of the general population stemmed from the fact that social and behavioral scientists have only recently come to the stage where they can now define the social and psychological attributes of individuals. Public libraries in particular have made exceptional gains in the area of designing information delivery systems. Community analysis of needs has been the most common method of analysis. Such demographic facts as age, ethnicity, income and education are still considered valid factors in planning information systems.

Population characteristics revealed in recent U.S. census data show that people live longer.[1] Men will live an average of age of 70 and women 75.5 years. This life expectancy is expected to increase in the coming decade. The psychological plus the physiological realities of aging need to be understood by planners. The elderly have basic information needs in the areas of housing, retirement, health care and social service benefits.

Racial, ethnic and cultural variables are still real considerations in planning information services. As an example, Spanish-speakers have become the largest linguistic minority and are one of the fastest growing population groups. A special task force appointed by the National Commission on Libraries and Information Science indicated racial minorities are still being underserved by many information agencies.

In the case of rural populations it is expected that the tax base will continue to be eroded by the drop in farm prices. There is a continuing rural to urban shift in population in some parts of the country. In other rural areas the median age falls in the mid-twenties. Agencies serving rural areas will have to be alert to finding out continuing information needs of a changing rural population.

DERVIN'S FINDINGS

Dervin's research[2] assesses information needs of potential clientele by examining individuals in the context of their own lives. Described as sense-making, this research approach looks at individual information needs outside of systems of information. The focus is on problems rather than questions. Other more traditional approaches to information needs look at individuals in terms of a system e.g., library or information center. The traditional approach is content driven and is based on need related to subject. Dervin's sense-making approach to studying information needs asks people "What kinds of situations were you in which required your attention?" "What kinds of questions did you have in these situations?" and "What kind of help did you hope to get from answers to your questions?" This approach draws out the implications for information service. Traditional needs studies ask "When was the last time you visited a public library?" "What is your source for job information?" "Did you find what you wanted at the library?" McMullin and Taylor give a word of caution that sense-making is not sufficiently understood at present to be used in designing information systems. "Rather it depends on that large class of interpreters endemic in the information society called consultants, counselors, instructors, etc."[3]

Some of the implications from Dervin's work are as follows:

1. Librarians need to put more emphasis on the human dimensions of information use. Providing access means more than making information available. It requires that information have 'useability.' Application for libraries would include finding ways to select and organize resources which are determined relevant by users, especially "for making connections to their own lives." This also has implications for the reference interview. Clients should be encouraged to fully relate "in their own terms" the kinds of help they are seeking. Catalogers and collection developers might have to include in the organization of resources some of these more personal descriptions and categorizations of needs.

2. The information poor and the information rich differ in their life situations and the types of sense-making they do. A practical

realization in psychological terms is that the poor and alienated and the not so poor have different ways and schemes of making sense of their worlds.

There is still a great need for crisis lines and I & R services planned to meet basic human needs. Many of these services are no longer being provided by public libraries since the cutting of federal funds for library programs.

The interpersonal communication links that many individuals depend on for information should be fully utilized. As a tradition interpersonal links are strong among many groups. Utilizing the total communication environment of individuals (e.g., community networks, popular media) might be helpful.

3. Wherein demographic variables are important as noted above there is growing evidence that information and library systems should place less emphasis on demographic variables in planning and organizing services. In Dervin's work the demographic characteristics relate only to aspects of information seeking and use constrained by the same life conditions that demography indexes. On the other hand the sense-making approach shows that demography will not predict the subtle cognitive, internal types of sense-making. "Yet, library and information systems rely heavily on a variety of different demographic analysis of their communities. Clearly, these approaches have utility in some frames of reference." However, Dervin's work points to an important linkage between the individual's situation and the use that will be made of any information obtained. The sense-making approach shows that demographic variables alone will not predict the subtle cognitive, internal types of need fulfillment.

4. Information needs change constantly and libraries should design information services that are responsive to current needs assessments. Occasional needs assessment will not do, it is an activity that should be an ongoing, normal library activity. A library reference department or information system might make a weekly random sample of potential clientele a regular staff routine.

An important area needing more research is on the nature and dimensions of information McMullin and Taylor have identified traits which can be seen as intrinsic to information. They maintain that some traits exist on a continuum and others appear to be "dichotomous and naturally exclusive." These traits refer to such characteristics such as the following dichotomies: design/structure, assumptions explicit/not explicit, etc.[4]

Formulating a theory of information-seeking is still in process. It will be up to information specialists to use what is known and apply it to the creation of more efficient information delivery systems. Already it is suspected that future information systems for the general population will not be centered in isolated and traditional library systems. Is it possible there will be a new type of information providing system, separate from libraries? As an example, most information and referral systems today have evolved outside of libraries. Reference librarians must continue to establish linkages with other agencies mandated to provide information. Planners of information delivery systems will need to integrate client centered services into the total information environment which embraces all electronic and print media; government and social agencies; family; friends and community. *Everybody needs information.*

REFERENCES

1. Facigno, Kathleen and Polly Guynup. "U.S. Population Characteristics: Implications for Libraries." *Wilson Library Bulletin*, 59, 1, pp. 25-26.
2. Dervin, Brenda. "Information Sense-Making" Unpublished 1976.
3. McMullin, Susan and Robert S. Taylor. "Problem Dimension and Information Traits." *The Information Society*, 1984, 3, 1, p. 108.
4. McMullin, Susan and Robert S. Taylor. "Problem Dimension and Information Traits." *The Information Society*, 1984, 3, 1, pp. 102-107.

BIBLIOGRAPHY

Borman, Christopher. "Effectives of Reinforcement Style of Counseling on Information-Seeking Behavior." *Journal of Vocational Behavior*, 1972, 2, 255-259.
Clark, Peter and Jim James. "The Effects of Situation, Attitude Intensity and Personality in Information-Seeking." *Sociometry*. September 1967, 235-245.
Dervin, Brenda. *The Information Needs of Californians*. California State Library 1984.
Ducker, Kenneth. "Urban Information Systems and Urban Indicators." *Urban Affairs Quarterly*. 1970, December, 173-178.
Facigno, Kathleen, and Polly Guynup. "U.S. Population Characteristics: Implications for Libraries." *Wilson Library Bulletin*, 1984, 39, 1, pp. 23-26.
Harris, Jacqueline and Maxwell E. McCombs. "The Interpersonal Mass Communication Interface Among Church Leaders." *The Journal of Communication*. September 1972, 257-262.
Jackson, Miles M. *Mass Communication Behavior in Washington, D.C.* Ph.D. Dissertation, Syracuse University, 1974.
Katz, Elihu. "The Two-Step Flow of Communication." *Public Opinion Quarterly*. Spring 1957, 61-78.
Levin, James, Nathan Brody. "Information Deprivation and Creativity." *Psychological Reports*. 1974, 231-237.

McMullin, Susan and Robert S. Taylor. "Problem Dimensions and Information Traits." *The Information Society.* 1984, 3, 1, pp. 91-111.
Robbins, Gerold E. "Dogmatism and Information Gathering in Personality Impression Formation," *Journal of Research in Personality.* 1975, 9, 74-78.
Rogers, Everett. *Communication of Innovations*, Free Press, 1984.
Taylor, Robert S. "Question-Negotiation and Information Seeking in Libraries." *College and Research Libraries.* May 1968, 178-194.
Warner, Edward, et al. *Information Needs of Urban Residents.* Final Report. U.S. Department of Health, Education and Welfare. OEC-NO-0-71- 4555, 1973.

Multiple Roles of Academic Reference Librarians: Problems of Education and Training

Barbara E. Kemp

A quick glance at the position announcements listed in a variety of professional journals reveals what most academic reference librarians have known for a long time: reference positions are among the most demanding professionally. While this, in part, may be due to the difficult but rewarding public service aspects of the work, I feel that the increasing diversity of roles that a reference librarian is asked to undertake adds immeasurably to the demands placed upon the individuals who fill these positions. William Miller recently has presented cogent arguments against the unplanned proliferation of various reference-related services;[1] yet even without expanded services, an up-to-date, professionally active academic reference librarian is usually asked to wear several professional hats. This in itself can be difficult for entry-level librarians, who often are not accustomed to juggling multiple demands for their time. The problem becomes more acute when one realizes the widely different nature of the roles these librarians are asked to fill, and the corresponding competencies or skills that are necessary to perform adequately.

What are these roles that are so diverse? First and foremost is the provision of direct reference service to patrons. This role may be further refined to include the roles of generalist and specialist. Responsibility for online searching often rests with the reference department, as does the provision of all levels of bibliographic instruction. In many cases, reference librarians are also responsible for collection development. While this duty usually is tied to an individual's reference subject specialty, it is a rare library that has a qualified specialist for every subject. In most cases, librarians are assigned several subject areas of collection development responsi-

---

The author is Head, Humanities/Social Sciences Public Services, Washington State University, Pullman, WA 99164.

© 1986 by The Haworth Press, Inc. All rights reserved.

bility. If they are lucky, the subject areas may be related; but all too often, beginning librarians must accept subject areas in which they have little or no training. In addition to specific responsibilities related to the collection, the subject specialist usually has faculty liaison responsibilities. The role of supervisor does not seem to appear as often in advertisements for entry-level positions, but studies indicate that this role may be more common than might be expected.[2] Beyond this set of position-related roles, an academic reference librarian must be prepared to serve on various library committees and task forces. At the same time there is an expectation that the librarian will function as a member of the broader academic community. This is most often accomplished by serving on a variety of campus-wide committees.

Although this list of roles or responsibilities assigned to reference librarians is impressive in itself, it should be emphasized that these are roles identified by scanning recent position announcements. While it is possible that such diversity is not asked of all reference librarians, it is equally possible that, in some situations, even more roles may be assigned.

What then are the competencies or skills necessary for a librarian to perform well in all of the above roles? According to one writer,

> Reference librarianship requires not only the pursuit of encyclopedic knowledge and the practice of a systematic research methodology, but also the skills of a diplomat, the counseling ability of a psychologist, and the physical and emotional stamina of an Olympic athlete . . . hard-pressed librarians must be able to think fast, keep their 'cool,' and demonstrate strong social welfare instincts. A pronounced sense of humor helps to ward off symptoms of battle fatigue.[3]

Obviously there is no substitute for the reference librarian's solid grasp of bibliographic methods and tools. The ability to follow a systematic search strategy and make use of appropriate resources in daily reference work is essential to provide good service. This same knowledge is important in online searching, since a searcher must be aware of both printed sources and online databases and must be able to apply analytical skills in designing a search strategy. A bibliographic instruction librarian must also be familiar with a wide variety of reference sources and be able to create a logical search strategy.

In-depth knowledge of one or more subject areas is a valuable asset for academic reference librarians. Subject specialists act as resources for their colleagues and other researchers in dealing with difficult questions. A proper mix of subject specialists can form an extremely effective reference team. The value of a subject specialty carries over to many of the other roles of the reference librarian. Online searchers often specialize in a group of subject-related databases, and subject specialists are called upon to provide bibliographic instruction in specific disciplines. Familiarity with the literature of a discipline improves the librarian's ability to make informed and balanced judgments when selecting materials for the general collection.

Understanding technical services operations is important both to reference service and to collection development. As the interpreter of the library and its holdings, the reference librarian should be aware of acquisitions procedures and have "a thorough understanding of both past and current cataloging principles and practices."[4] Unfortunately, many reference librarians do not take time to really understand the card catalog and its use as a reference tool, being satisfied instead with knowing enough "to get along." However, as online catalogs are developed, it becomes increasingly important for reference librarians to be involved in their design. There is an opportunity to create many user-friendly approaches to the catalog, improving service and making reference work easier. Online searchers in particular may be able to suggest attractive system features. Yet without sufficient knowledge of cataloging, reference librarians' contributions to the process can remain largely ineffective. One must understand the product that one is trying to improve.

Familiarity with one or more of the commercially available online systems, such as DIALOG or BRS, has become an important skill for most reference librarians. It is, of course, absolutely essential if one is to execute the searches, but some knowledge of these systems should be required of all reference librarians. Anyone working at the reference desk should be able to recognize potential online search questions and make appropriate referrals or be able to answer basic questions asked by users.

As bibliographic instruction becomes more sophisticated, librarians are refining their skills in this area. To be effective teachers, they are studying various learning theories in order to establish a conceptual basis for instruction programs. In addition to this theoretical knowledge, bibliographic instruction librarians are expected to be able to plan and deliver presentations to classes, as well as to produce a variety of instructional materials.

If reference librarians are expected to supervise others, even student assistants, they must become familiar with the personnel policies and procedures of the institution. However, their effectiveness as supervisors will increase if they understand and are able to apply some basic management principles concerning supervision, budgeting, and planning.

A final set of competencies needed for successful reference librarianship deals with the broad area of human relations skills. At times these skills seem to be classified under the generic label of "communication skills," but the totality is really much more complex. Reference librarians need to be able to speak and write clearly. These skills are essential if one is expected to work with the public and interpret the library for its users. They are equally important to the roles of online searcher, bibliographic instruction librarian, collection development specialist and supervisor.

Reference librarians also should possess counseling and interviewing skills, including the ability to be an active listener. It is also helpful to possess sensitivity to others, especially in terms of cultural differences. As members of a reference department and "team," reference librarians should be skilled in the area of group dynamics. This skill also increases one's effectiveness as a committee member.

A summarized list of these competencies is no less impressive than the list of roles the librarian must play: (1) knowledge of research methodology; (2) general knowledge of information sources; (3) in-depth subject knowledge; (4) understanding of technical services operations, including cataloging and acquisitions; (5) knowledge of one or more commercially available online search systems; (6) teaching ability; (7) management skills; (8) articulateness; (9) counseling skills; (10) sensitivity; (11) group dynamics skills.

In reviewing this admittedly partial list of competencies, administrators might well engage in some soul-searching. In creating positions with so many different responsibilities, requiring different talents and kinds of education and training, are we creating situations that can lead to personnel and service problems?

Although many reference librarians are attracted to the field precisely by the opportunity for varied job responsibilities, it is unlikely that many entry-level librarians have been adequately prepared in all the needed competencies. A survey of library directors has shown that although human relations, analytical, and computer application and retrieval skills are desired competencies, "entry-level librarians were evaluated as satisfactorily prepared only in the bibliographic areas."[5] A Delphi technique study of the roles and functions of academic public services librarians in the future has foreseen "a wide range of skills, including . . . communication and interpersonal relations skills, as growing in importance by the year 2000."[6]

Everyone suffers if librarians do not have the skills necessary to perform their jobs well. Service deteriorates when reference librarians cannot answer questions and are unable to communicate. What reference librarian has not had the experience of working with a very knowledgeable colleague who was unable to communicate that knowledge to the public and truly share his or her expertise? Users are dissatisfied when online searches are poorly designed, executed, and explained. Students and faculty alike become alienated if they are exposed to poorly designed and delivered presentations or instructional materials. A supervising librarian with no management skills can quickly create chaos leading to further deterioration of services and alienation of the staff.

More, however, is involved in a librarian's inadequate preparation than the direct harm done to service. Also to be considered are the possible effects on the staff as a whole and on the librarian personally. Frustration and resentment are likely outcomes if other librarians are repeatedly called upon to "cover" for the ill-prepared librarian. Similarly, people caught in jobs for which they have not been adequately prepared will experience feelings of frustration, resentment, and most probably, some degree of guilt. These feelings, combined with normal day-to-day job pressures, will often lead to some degree of burnout.

The deleterious effects on service and staff can be devastating to the library. "Personnel failure is more costly to the organization than is generally recognized and replacement is far more costly than finding the right task or developing right skills."[7]

One might well ask why administrators hire people who are not qualified for positions. One answer is that there are probably relatively few people who possess all the competencies and skills outlined, especially if they are new graduates. Additional factors are that many of the desired qualifications are implicit rather than explicit, others are grouped under broad labels such as "communication skills" or "teaching ability," and, sadly enough, still others are assumed to be natural products of an education.

It is this last assumption which I find particularly naive. Although it might be hoped that students have acquired analytical skills somewhere along the line in their studies, most of us realize that this is not necessarily the case. Similarly, having managed to acquire two or more degrees does not magically endow a person with real communication, interpersonal, or teaching skills. There are some people for whom these are natural talents, but it is far more common to study and learn them in formal classroom situations. It somehow seems presumptuous to assume that a library science student can learn interviewing skills as part of one course in reference when students in other helping professions usually develop these skills much more intensively through full-length courses and actual field work. In the same vein, library science students may study bibliographic instruction as part of a course or may even have one course devoted to the subject, yet education students follow a succession of courses and do student teaching in order to develop "teaching ability."

Although I personally would like to see library school programs counsel students who are interested in reference librarianship more effectively, it is not my intent simply to fire another salvo in the continuing war between library practitioners and educators. I am more interested in pointing out what might be termed irrational expectations for entry-level librarians. As Herbert White put it, "In librarianship, however, we somehow expect to hire people at 9 a.m., send them through personnel indoctrination, and turn them loose on the backlog [or reference desk] at 10 a.m."[8]

If administrators approve positions requiring so many different skills of one person, then they ought to assume some responsibility to the person who is hired, as well as being aware of the consequences of failure.

> Before even advertising a position opening, the supervisor should list the areas of competency that a fully functioning staff member is required to master for that position. Then the supervisor should decide which of these competencies can reasonably be learned in the context of the work environment. All other competencies should become minimum qualifications for that position.[9]

If administrators knowingly hire someone who is not adequately prepared for a position and there is no intention of providing needed training, then they are either setting the new librarian up for failure or tacitly agreeing to potentially diminished service.

At this point the question of staff development versus continuing education, must be raised. There is a strong, continuing debate in the profession as to the nature of post-MLS education and training, and with whom the responsibility for providing it rests. There are those who say that any lack in a librarian's formal education should be identified by the librarian, who is also responsible for correcting that lack. However, there are others who contend that "Staff development is primarily concerned with the needs on the job and takes over where preemployment training stops."[10] In this view, it is in the best interests of the library to provide adequate training for a job. To this I would add that it is only ethical to do so in light of the kinds of positions we create.

Up until now, I have focused on the plight of the entry-level librarian. It is important, however, to recognize that reference librarians at all levels of experience could be encountering the same problems. It is even possible that the more experienced librarians are not even aware that a problem exists. Although some might feel that experienced librarians should bear the responsibility for upgrading their skills as part of their professional development, I would argue that some skills are so basic to the provision of good service, that the organizaton bears at least equal responsibility for any retraining or up-grading necessary. It has been pointed out that it seems easier to accept and pay for depreciation on expensive equipment like computers than it is to accept and pay for needed upgrading of skills.[11] This view is common, but it shows a basic lack of understanding that people are probably the most important of the library's resources.

There are many alternatives for helping librarians acquire needed skills. There has been a proliferation of workshops and seminars, with a heavy emphasis on the areas of online searching and bibliographic instruction. Of course, these offerings often carry a rather hefty price tag, which discourages participation. It is even more costly if one includes the cost of travel, lodging, meals, etc. One way of amortizing these costs is to require anyone attending to give a formal report to the other reference staff members upon returning. This approach not only has the advantage of sharing the information gathered but also allows the librarian a chance to hone various communication skills and helps in building the "team" concept. Another way to reduce the costs of workshops is by offering to serve as the host institution. Often, the host is allowed one or more free registrations.

Tapping the expertise on campus is another valuable source of training that is often overlooked. Institutional personnel departments usually have some programs that can be helpful, especially in the areas of supervision and some communications skills. Academic departments which teach courses related to the helping professions, psychology, and education can be contacted for help in developing one-time presentations or full training programs.

Naturally, no administrator should overlook the expertise that exists on the reference staff. It is common practice for new librarians to learn more about reference sources by working with their more experienced colleagues. This same kind of on-the-job training takes place with other skills too, but to be really effective it should be more formalized. Reference staff meetings can be a forum for all to share their frustrations, successes, ways of dealing with problems, etc. If certain problem areas are identified, different librarians can research them and report back to the group for wider discussion. Self-instruction and group sharing should be actively encouraged.

These are only some of the ways that new skills can be acquired and old ones upgraded. As I have indicated, I feel that the administration bears a great deal of responsibility for the provision of adequate training, but it should be remembered that the reference librarians themselves share in the responsibility. They must be willing to identify honestly those areas in which they lack adequate preparation and work with the administration in creating educational and training opportunities to correct that lack. Librarians must also be willing to take advantage of the opportunities provided and work to learn new skills or refurbish old ones. Once the desired competencies are acquired, a professional has the responsibility for maintaining them and sharing them with others.

REFERENCES

1. William Miller, "What's Wrong with Reference: Coping with Success and Failure at the Reference Desk," *American Libraries*, 15(5): 303-306, 321-322.

2. Gemma DeVinney and Patricia Tegler, "Preparation for Academic Librarianship: a Survey," *College and Research Libraries*, 44(3): 223-227; also Ralph M. Edwards, *The Role of the Beginning Librarian in University Libraries*, ACRL Publications in Librarianship, no. 37, (Chicago: American Library Association, 1975).

3. Ann T. Hinckley, "The Reference Librarian," *College and Research Libraries News*, 41(3): 62-63.

4. Diana M. Thomas, Ann T. Hinckley, and Elizabeth R. Eisenbach, *The Effective Reference Librarian*, (New York: Academic Press, 1981): p. 192.

5. Richard M. Dougherty and Wendy P. Lougee, "Research Library Residencies: a New Model for Professional Development," *Library Journal*, 108(12): 1323.

6. Theophil M. Otto, "The Academic Librarian of the 21st Century: Public Service and Library Education in the Year 2000," *The Journal of Academic Librarianship*, 8(2): 88.

7. Murray S. Martin, *Issues In Personnel Management in Academic Libraries*, (Greenwich, Conn.: JAI Press, 1981): 141.

8. Herbert S. White, "Defining Basic Competencies," *American Libraries*, 14(8): 520.

9. David R. Dowell, "The Role of the Supervisor in Training and Developing Staff," in Allerton Park Institute, 24th, 1978, *Supervision of Employees in Libraries*, ed. Rolland E. Stevens (Urbana-Champaign: University of Illinois, Graduate School of Library Science, 1978): 62.

10. Martin, p. 144.

11. Martin, p. 141.

The Recruitment, Selection and Retention of Academic Reference Librarians

Ilene F. Rockman

Although academic librarianship has gradually moved toward shared responsibility and increased participation in management policy and decision making, particularly in personnel matters, no consummate body of literature currently exists on the topic of the recruitment, selection, and retention of academic reference librarians.[1] The purpose of this article, therefore, is to suggest salient factors which can contribute to successful employment practices in college and university libraries.

A clear understanding of the role and function of a reference librarian must come prior to the writing of any job description, advertisement, or recruitment strategy. This understanding may include the identification of desirable thinking skills, personality characteristics, academic requirements, and relevant experience.

CHARACTERISTICS OF A REFERENCE LIBRARIAN

The literature is replete with position papers and opinions on the qualities of a successful reference librarian.[2] Often these opinions focus upon educational training and personality characteristics—whether academic librarians should be generalistics or specialists, and whether the reference process should be source or client-centered—rather than on an overriding philosophy of reference librarianship.

If a library subscribes to the notion of counselor-librarianship popularized at the University of Pittsburgh,[3] the emphasis on applicants who can display cognitive flexibility, communication con-

---

The author is Associate Librarian, California Polytechnic State University, San Luis Obispo, CA 93407.

© 1986 by The Haworth Press, Inc. All rights reserved.

sistency, perceptual sensitivity, and interpersonal involvement may influence the wording of the position description, the interview process, and the type of individual selected for the position. If, on the other hand, the scholar-librarian image is subscribed to,[4] the emphasis on research competence and publication requirements may instead gain prominence in the advertisement, selection, and appointment. Or, if the library encourages inter-departmental or dual job assignments,[5] greater emphasis may be placed upon applicants who are flexible and possess a wide sphere of skill in both public and technical services. Lastly, if the library believes that the role of the reference librarian is "to teach users how to find their own information . . . (and) to supply information in response to stated needs,"[6] then the advertisement needs to reflect this instructional role.

The ability to skillfully negotiate questions, the knowledge of how and when to gently probe for more information while in a reference encounter, the quiet tenacity to pursue a question until an answer is found, and the quickness of mind to effectively handle several questions are not easy traits to recognize. Yet, if these are priorities of reference service, they should be explicitly stated in any recruitment, selection, or appointment activities.

Moreover, also important to specify and clarify are the responsibilities and demands of the reference position. These may include reference desk assistance, online searching, bibliographic instruction, collection development, faculty outreach, and/or preparation of instructional materials. Demands for flexibility required to juggle these varied assignments within a changing weekly schedule should also be recognized.

A clear picture of the library's reference philosophy and the requisite responsibilities in priority order are necessary to identify before the recruitment process can begin.

RECRUITMENT

Recruitment is the process by which the widest qualified applicant pool is attracted to an open position. Recent changes in academic librarian recruitment processes have been attributed to the adoption of policies of shared responsibilities by using the committee structure to encourage various points of view[7] and federal legislation requiring adherence to affirmative action/equal employment opportunity guidelines.[8] As a result, it is now common practice to see some form of librarian participation in the academic recruitment process which was once the sole purview of library administrators.

Given the fact that many libraries believe in the concept of a committee, particularly for a national search, the first step in the recruitment process is the constitution of such a committee. Individuals may be appointed by the library administration or elected by peers; represent the entire library, the public services area, or the department/branch with the vacancy. They may serve as a search, screen, or search and screen committee; select sources for the advertisement; write and place the advertisement; approve the recruitment budget; receive, assess, and check references; draft interview schedules and questions; make final recommendations; rank recommended candidates; or fulfill a combination of these functions. Often the position to be filled will influence the size and composition of the committee, and administrative librarians may serve as voting or non-voting members often to handle correspondence, supervise record-keeping, and offer procedural guidance. Whatever the responsibilities, the value of a search committee is often the range of expertise and experience that members bring to the process[9] in an attempt to facilitate objective consideration of each candidate's qualifications.[10]

Once the committee is constituted and has a charge, it must determine a realistic time frame in which to operate. This is especially important in national searches which require time to seek nominations; advertise in widely-read library publications (e.g., *American Libraries, College and Research Libraries News*), non-library publications, (e.g., *The New York Times, The Chronicle of Higher Education*), and minority publications (e.g., *The Black Scholar, Affirmative Action Register*); contact association telephone hotlines; mail announcements to graduate library schools, library directors, and personnel administrators at similar institutions; and recruit at conference placement centers and reference-oriented meetings, workshops, and seminars.

Advertisements should clearly delineate the job title and rank; major responsibilities and reporting structure; educational training required or desired; years of experience; application procedures (e.g., names of three references or letters to accompany the resume, library school placement file to be sent, graduate transcripts and degree verification required); health and vacation benefits; minimum salary or salary range; information about the university and surrounding community; and closing date. Ideally, as each candidate's inquiry arrives, an acknowledgment letter should be sent from the library administrative office. This practice insures that all applicants are treated with equity, courtesy, and respect.

Because service on a committee can be an intensive and time consuming activity, before the closing date has arrived, committee members can meet to select a chair (if one has not been appointed), review the charge, establish procedures, and prioritize criteria upon which all applicants are to be fairly and consistently judged. They can also be alerted as applications arrive, so that initial independent assessments can occur. Preliminary planning can save valuable time once the position has closed and the full process begins to unfold.

SELECTION

Within seven to ten days after the closing date, the committee can meet again. This meeting can focus upon a preliminary discussion of the applicants in an attempt to identify those candidates who do not meet the minimum requirements for the position and will need to be sent regret letters. Remaining candidates can be assigned low or high ratings, notified that they are still under consideration, and, if necessary, actively encouraged to complete their files. Those persons clearly at the top of the consideration list can be telephoned to ascertain their continued interest and if warranted, to arrange for a pre-screening telephone interview.

The committee can then meet to coordinate its questions, review any library guidelines on conducting pre-employment interviews, and clarify its commitment to the confidentiality of each file.

If it is determined that telephone interviews will occur, it is advantageous to conduct them in a private office on a conference line so that all members have the benefit of hearing the questions and answers. For consistency, one individual can take responsibility for introductions and asking the questions. Members can funnel any written follow-up questions to the speaker for clarification or elaboration. Sufficient time should be allowed for the candidate to pose questions to the committee, and before the interview has concluded, the applicant should have a clear understanding of the percentage of time allocated to each of the reference duties described in the position advertisement, the library's philosophy of reference service, and the performance standards associated with the position. In addition, the committee should be able to judge the relevance of the candidate's experience, education, and intellectual abilities in relation to the job requirements.[11]

As the process evolves, the committee can decide which candidates to invite for on-campus interviews based upon the telephone experience. Responsibilities for travel, housing, and entertainment arrangements should be discussed, and candidates should be informed if they will need to assume part of the expenses. They should be advised if telephone reference checks will occur and, prior to coming to campus, be sent an interview schedule and information about the library, the college or university, and the local community.

An announcement about applicants scheduled to be interviewed should be communicated to the library staff, and a copy of each candidates resume can be made available to interested staff members.

Opportunities for the candidates to tour the library and meet with professional and support staffs should be part of the interview day. Committee members can also provide time for the candidates to speak with the library director and reference department head. At each of these meetings, care should be taken to provide the candidate with new information and not to ask repetitive questions. For example, the committee can focus upon the job within the setting of the entire library; the department head on the specifics of the job; the assistant director or personnel librarian on benefits and the community; and the library director on tenure and promotion practices, salary, and personal goals. Because a telephone interview has already occurred, each experience can concentrate on open-ended, in-depth questions in an attempt to assess each candidates qualifications in relation to the needs and requirements of the position.

Committee members can also schedule time for the candidate to meet with faculty members, deliver a prepared address to library staff members, or work at the reference desk all in an attempt to assess the capabilities of the candidate of fulfilling the requirements of the position.

Once all potential candidates have been interviewed, the committee can deliberate and rank preferences. Sensitivity to affirmative action and equal employment opportunity guidelines should be taken into consideration. Written decisions of the committee should be forwarded to the library director, or if appropriate, to the chair of the tenured librarians. Responsibility for contract negotiations, salary, starting date, and notifying unsuccessful candidates, however, rests with the library director.

RETENTION

Retention or reappointment, indicates to a librarian that satisfactory progress has been achieved in fulfilling performance standards. The process permits a mechanism for periodic and systematic review with opportunities to extend incentives or rewards (intrinsic or extrinsic) for valued performance and service. Just as recruitment and selection activities involve participation by non-administrative personnel, so does the process of performance appraisal.

Often a peer review committee, as well as the immediate supervisor and the library director, may be involved in the evaluation process for retention. Criteria for judging performance by these groups should be consistent and may include effectiveness as both a reference librarian and a team librarian, scholarly contributions, professional activities, service to the university and community involvement. These criteria "may be weighted to reflect the importance of (each) area."[12]

Candidates may prepare self-assessment documents on which to be judged to assist, guide, and focus the written comments of the committee. These documents may also be supplemented by letters from faculty, students, and library colleagues.

Some libraries divide evaluation responsibilities into two parts—peer evaluation for reappointment, tenure, and promotion considerations, and supervisory appraisal for performance improvements and salary determination.[13] This system may be useful in those instances when the peer review committee members may come from areas other than the reference department or public services area. Other librarians may assign greater value to the comments of the peer review committee or treat all evaluations equally. Whatever the balance, the criteria upon which the reference librarian is to be evaluated for retention should be attainable and in harmony with the goals and philosophy of the reference department. Such criteria may include an awareness of new reference titles, the knowledge of how a discipline is bibliographically controlled, courtesy and patience when dealing with patrons, an attitude which encourages patrons to approach the reference desk, and capable reference search techniques.[14]

For those librarians who are performing above the standard, appreciation can be extended through salary adjustments or increased responsibility. The notion of job enrichment, enlargement, or redesign is a useful option, particularly when budgetary conditions do not permit adequate financial compensation for a job well done; the library wants to boost the morale or job satisfaction of a deserving librarian; the librarian needs specialized skills or a change in title to pursue and attain personal goals; or the library wants to retain a valued employee and is willing to increase the sphere and complexity of the present job assignments to do so.

CONCLUSION

Although no definitive body of literature exists on the subject of the recruitment, selection, and retention of academic reference librarians, recognition and awareness of this gap can assist in filling it.

Provocative discussions and challenging articles urging the profession to study personnel issues in the hope of determining appropriate performance appraisal measures for reference librarians have recently appeared.[15]

Until such time, however, as uniform techniques are established and adopted, each library is faced with the individual task of attracting, selecting, and retaining quality personnel. Clear library goals, an identifiable reference service philosophy, and consistent evaluation practices may assist in this endeavor.

REFERENCES

1. Although not specific to reference librarians, a good compilation of policy documents can be found in *Recruitment Practices in ARL Libraries: Spec Kit 78*. Washington, D.C.: Association of Research Libraries, October 1981; see also Christine Matthews et al. "Recruitment of Academic Librarians." *Behavioral and Social Sciences Librarian* 1 (Winter 1979): 138; see also Lawrence J. Heilos et al. *University of South Florida Libraries Search Committee Procedure Handbook*. Tampa: University of South Florida, 1981. ERIC ED 224485.

2. Samuel Rothstein. "The Making of a Reference Librarian." *Library Trends* 31 (Winter 1983): 375-99; Arthur Ray Roland. *The Librarian and Reference Service*. Hamden, CT: The Shoe String Press, 1977.

3. Patrick R. Penland. *Interviewing for Counselor and Reference Librarian*. Preliminary Edition. Pittsburgh: University of Pittsburgh, 1970; Patrick R. Penland. "Counselor Librarianship." *Encyclopedia of Library and Information Science*. V. 6. (New York; Dekker, 1971) pp. 240-54.

4. LeMoyne W. Anderson. "Librarians as Scholars." *Academic Librarianship: Yesterday, Today, and Tomorrow*. (New York: Neal-Schuman, 1982) pp. 161-79.

5. Laurie S. Linsley. "The Dual Job Assignment: How It Enhances Job Satisfaction." *Proceedings of the Third National Conference of the Association of College and Research Libraries*, (Seattle: ACRL 1984) pp. 146-50.

6. F. William Summers. "Education for Reference Service." *The Service Imperative for Libraries: Essays in Honor of Margaret E. Monroe.* (Littleton, CO: Libraries Unlimited, 1982) p. 63.

7. John F. Harvey and May Parr. "University Library Search and Screen Committees." *College and Research Libraries* 37 (July 1976): 347.

8. Sheila Creth. "Recruitment: Planning for Success." *Drexel Library Quarterly* 17 (Summer 1981): 52-55.

9. Creth, p. 65.

10. "Guidelines and Procedures for the Screening and Appointment of Academic Librarians." *College and Research Libraries News* 38 (September 1977): 231.

11. Richard A. Fear. *The Evaluation Interview.* 2nd ed. (New York: McGraw-Hill, 1978) p. 24.

12. Maxine Reneker. "Performance Appraisal in Libraries: Purpose and Techniques." *Personnel Administration in Libraries.* (New York: Neal-Schuman, 1981) p. 261.

13. Reneker, p. 265.

14. William F. Young. "Evaluating the Reference Librarian." *The Reference Librarian* 11 (Fall/Winter 1984): p. 127.

15. Charles Martell. "Editorial: Performance at the Reference Desk." *College and Research Libraries* 46 (January 1985): pp. 3-4.

Reference Librarians as Teachers: Ego, Ideal and Reality in a Reference Department

Ellen Broidy

The question of burnout has become an extremely popular subject amongst academic reference librarians.[1] More often than not, we engage in heated debate about the causes of burnout, actively seeking out villians upon whom to lay the blame for our distress. Much less frequently heard are ideas about how to stem the negative tide once it has begun, or creative solutions designed to prevent the appearance of the burnout monster in our midst. The litany of reasons offered for this apparently highly prevalent malady often includes, overtly or covertly, the stresses and strains that accompany active bibliographic instruction programs. Somehow the effort to expand traditional definitions of reference service and to enrich and enhance professional opportunities for individual librarians (not to mention improving the quality of life for our students) by integrating library instruction activities into a general reference program is having the opposite effect. Let me suggest that the problems we are facing with respect to burnout may have little to do with what we are trying to accomplish when we encourage the development and growth of instruction programs. The difficulties we encounter may well lie in how we are going about it.

Poor allocation of personnel resources poses as serious a problem as inadequate resources. While I hesitate to recommend that libraries, or more specifically reference services, make do, there comes a point where our energies must be directed towards dealing with present realities. In terms of the impact of library instruction on traditional library and reference services, that moment is clearly upon us. The perceived adverse effects of new or different or expanded service must be analyzed from the perspective of carefully

---

The author is Coordinator of Library Education Services, General Library, University of California at Irvine, CA 92713.

© 1986 by The Haworth Press, Inc. All rights reserved.

considered allocation of available personnel resources. The personnel issues that most often affect the delivery of quality library instruction services fall into four main areas:

1. administration of the library instruction program;
2. recruitment, interviewing, and hiring of instruction librarians (or, librarians with an instruction component to their jobs);
3. training and evaluation of instruction librarians;
4. decisions about which librarians should teach.

All of these areas are sensitive because they call into question institutional and programmatic priorities as well as individual professional self-image and academic judgement. The point of this discussion is to describe situations rather than prescribe solutions. Although each library is unique, each situation different, both the questions and the potential solutions are common enough to permit a degree of generalization.

ADMINISTRATION OF INSTRUCTION PROGRAMS

Administration of an instruction program is important not only for the quality and survival of the program, but also because various administrative configurations bring particular personnel issues to the fore. There are several different possible models for program administration, ranging from the creation of a separate and independent library instruction department to incorporation of the instructional activities as one functional area in a department, most often but not exclusively the reference department. Rather than join the ongoing debate on how to manage bibliographic instruction most effectively (a debate now celebrating more than a decade of non-resolution) let me simply sketch out some alternative models of program administration, highlighting the personnel issues (or consequences) inherent in each.

The Committee Approach

When libraries first become actively involved in the effort to provide bibliographic instruction to students (and faculty and staff), the program, in this nascent phase, is often coordinated by a library or bibliographic instruction committee. The committee may draw its membership from throughout the library, attracting both individuals committed to library instruction and those who feel they need a place to become involved—in any activity. Coordination through the committee structure should mean that the actual responsibility for provision of BI is shared amongst various librarians representing most, if not all, departments in the library. In some instances, the committee structure works admirably; the workload is truly shared, and technical services librarians with teaching ability and the desire to engage in this aspect of public service join their colleagues in providing instruction to the campus community. On the negative side, the committee approach may prevent the development of a true program, as the direction and philosophy must change with each shift in membership. Administration by committee is less successful as the program grows, communication may be difficult and coordination impossible.

The major reason for the lack of success with this administrative model emerges as a personnel issue. Although on paper all interested librarians share equally in the joys (and pitfalls) of library instruction, the reality is that public service librarians have the majority of opportunities for contact with faculty as well as the necessary familiarity with users' research difficulties. In addition, there is the problem of technical services department heads questioning the involvement of their staff in labor-intensive activities unrelated to traditional functional areas. The burden begins to fall more and more onto reference librarians who find that they are sharing "authority" for the program's direction, but shouldering the work alone.

The committee structure, designed initially to help get a fledgling program off the ground while fostering greater library-wide cooperation for the new effort, often has the reverse effect. Librarians may become less inclined to involve themselves in a new or different activity, particularly if department heads and administrators view these activities as ones which create conflicting demands on personnel.

Reference Department Responsibility

The assignment of responsibility to a particular department, usually reference, often evolves as the second stage in the administrative development of library instruction programs. Many reference departments, upon receiving the call for instruction or initiating it, create a functional area within the department and appoint one individual as coordinator.

This particular administrative model may have a profound impact on the library instruction program, the reference department and personnel throughout the library. Once instruction is situated in a particular department, the message sent to (or received by) the rest of the library is that bibliographic instruction is now territorial, the private preserve of one group of librarians. This, in and of itself, is not altogether negative. The nature of reference work, the daily contact with both users and sources, creates a "natural" base from which to build and refine instructional skills. But, ability at the desk does not always translate into ability in a classroom setting, and conversely, lack of public service experience does not automatically spell failure as a teacher.[2]

The incorporation of instruction into the functional duties of a reference department, while adding a dimension or at least an expectation to the librarians in that department, may rob others of the opportunity to teach. Department heads as well as upper level administrators may now point to reference, and its sole responsibility for intruction, whenever a librarian from another area expresses an interest in the activity. Instruction runs the risk of becoming an issue of territoriality, enforced more from outside the reference department than from within.

At this point instruction as a contributing factor in reference librarian burnout becomes apparent. As instruction programs grow, reference librarians, feeling overburdened and alone, may begin to perceive themselves as victims of their own successes. In recent years, with the advent of online catalogs and other changes in the technological face of the library, the growing need to respond to increasingly diverse student populations, and the necessity of expanding the definition of library instruction to include in-service training programs for library staff, it's no wonder reference department centered instruction programs are feeling the pinch—and succumbing to the burnout monster.

Independent Coordination

The third stage in my evolutionary theory of administrative models often comes about because the pressures on a particular department become too great, threatening the viability and vitality of the instruction program, not to mention the well-being of the reference librarians. As demands on an instruction program grow, the program may be in danger of having its philosophy, or goals, or mission determined externally. It may be difficult for a reference department, juggling a myriad of conflicting demands, to successfully manage or control an instruction program that incorporates not only traditional BI (tours, in-class lectures, etc.) but now must also respond to requests for in-service training for library staff, instruction in the use of online catalogs from campus administrators, and the successful integration of library instruction into dozens of required undergraduate courses. At this point, a library administration may wish to make an important, if delicate, personnel decision and remove coordination of library instruction from the reference department. Stage three sees the development of an independent office of library instruction.

This type of internal restructuring results immediately in a de-emphasis on reference as the sole providers of library instruction and possibly some relaxation of the strain reference librarians feel. In that respect this model is quite positive. On the other hand, coordination of a program from a separate office, physically as well as structurally, may create some unique personnel issues all its own. If the coordinator has programmatic responsibility but no direct supervisory function, what role, if any, may this individual play in evaluating the teaching performance and effectiveness of librarians? Responsibility without authority frequently proves to be a cause of dissatisfaction amongst middle managers. Coordinators who are not formally in management, yet are directly responsible for the quality of a library program, are apt to experience elevated levels of frustration as they strive to improve programs without having all the necessary resources and authority.

Evaluation, both of the program and its participants, is a key ingredient in the success of bibliographic instruction. The situation wherein a supervisor or department head "invites" evaluative commentary from a program coordinator is counterproductive to the instruction service. While a separate office probably performs the administrative activities (scheduling, communication, coordination) more successfully than either of the other two models, the personnel issues raised are less easily addressed.

Each of the three administrative models presented above creates unique personnel situations, many of them well beyond the scope of this article. Each of these three options, and there are others, does serve to underscore the need for each library to look critically at its own instruction program; determine the direction the program is taking, and who is taking it there. Weak or unsuccessful programs may result from lack of leadership. Leadership, as shown above, need not come from a single individual or even a single department, but the absence of a strong advocate (a committee chair, department head, program coordinator) for the librarians performing the instruction tasks contributes to the reference librarians' sense of isolation and feelings of burnout.

RECRUITING, INTERVIEWING, HIRING

Once, or when, or if, the question of program administration is resolved, the next personnel issue that must be addressed is recruiting, interviewing, and hiring of instruction librarians (or, librarians with an instruction component to their positions). The variety of types of instruction situations in academic libraries range from a position in a reference department in which librarians are expected to lead tours or provide orientation sessions to fully developed, administratively separate departments which recruit librarians specifically to teach. Rather than engage in a lengthy analysis of different librarian positions, let me instead discuss some possible methods which may be employed during recruitment and interview of candidates to assist in bringing the most qualified individual(s) to any instructional setting.[3]

Position announcements should emphasize the instruction component. The candidate must not read it as though it were put there as a trendy afterthought, or, even worse, feel that it may be ignored completely. Position announcements in professional journals are designed to transmit a great deal of information in a very little space. More care should be taken to spelling out the library's expectations. If instruction is an integral part of the job, it should be stated as such, with requirements fully outlined. For those institutions that can afford it, a separate position announcement detailing the instruction program should be prepared and forwarded to all serious applicants. Because of the wide variety of possible instruction programs and activities, the single statement "participation in bibliographic instruction" is insufficient. Applicants need information about the nature, scope, philosophy, and even the administration of the instruction program. While much of this may seem obvious, regrettably our personnel offices are still deluged with applications from individuals who are clearly unqualified for the position at hand and who have misread, or selectively read, the announcement.

The decision about who to invite for an interview is a major hurdle in the hiring process. A combination of factors including resume, cover letter, statement of qualifications (an oft neglected, very useful document), written and phone references, and the inevitable invisible networks combine to help us determine who to interview. Each component of this composite portrait of a potential employee must be scrutinized carefully. The library should be clear from the outset about its expectations, in terms of the job itself, the range of responsibilities and the level of appointment. With respect to the burnout factor, we need to take more care when we decide that a position with multiple, often conflicting responsibilities and pressures, is an entry level job. This is particularly true when dealing with library instruction which carries with it the added strain of teaching. Too often who we hire is determined by the level at which we can afford to hire rather than who will do the best job and suffer the least strain while doing it.

Applications from experienced librarians should look significantly different from those of entry level recent graduates. As we examine an applicant pool for an instruction job we must be willing to be analytical, critical, and read between the lines. Since few library schools offer courses specifically designed to teach librarians how to teach, transcripts prove less useful in determining skill or expertise (or experience) in this area. In the case of the recent graduate, the resume, statement of qualifications, and cover letter deserve careful attention. How much emphasis is the candidate putting on the instruction component? Did the candidate hold a teaching assistantship, either in library school or in another graduate program? Is there any evidence of membership in or attendance at organizations or programs focusing on bibliographic instruction? Just as those reading the various documents in support of a particular candidate must be diligent, the candidate must take care to highlight those points in her or his application.

Applications from more experienced librarians require another type of creative appraisal. Not only should the search committee examine the documents submitted, but someone needs to take the time to learn about the instruction program at the applicant's current library. Instruction programs vary widely, not only in the subjective areas of quality, but also in scope and quantity. No single philosophy unites us in assessing elements that make for a quality instruction program. Different institutions employ various methods, some of which are mutually exclusive. We owe it to our program to be as knowledgeable as possible about our candidates and their institutional experiences.

The Interview

Once the decision about who to interview has been made, the next step is to determine how to interview. This is somewhat more complicated if the open position is only partially instruction; here the issue becomes how best to integrate the instruction component into a crowded interview day, without losing sight of its importance. Since interviewing for a combined reference/instruction librarian position is a fairly typical situation, there are three general formats that a search committee or interview team might consider when interviewing a candidate for this particular split (or combined) assignment:

1. incorporate questions about library instruction into the general question and answer format;
2. ask the candidate to prepare a brief presentation on a particular reference source—frequently referred to as "teaching a tool;"
3. have the candidate outline a full instruction session in response to a scenario presented to the candidate in advance.

Option three, the scenario, though requiring the most effort on all parts, probably reveals the most and thus is the most productive. The candidate is sent an instruction situation or scenario, usually in the same mailing in which she or he receives the schedule for the interview day. The scenario should illustrate, as closely as possible, a situation the candidate might actually encounter in your institution. This has the advantage of providing the candidate with some information about your library while ensuring that the search committee may knowledgeably judge what it is hearing. Keep the scenario short, simple and relevant to the position in question. In other words, construct the scenario to the specifications of the job and the institution.

The scenario allows the candidate an opportunity to creatively explore issues in bibliographic instruction while at the same time provides enough structure so that the interviewers (or audience) may judge the candidate's ability to organize and present information.

An interview is one part of a complex and competitive personnel process. The candidate of the moment is aware that her or his performance is either being compared to yesterday's or filed away for future comparison. We continually search for objective standards against which to measure each candidate, yet far too often fall back on reliance upon the element of surprise, how well the individual performs under fire (or, to put it more politely, how well they "think on their feet"), answering a barrage of interview questions. But this provides only part of the picture and frequently the candidate and the committee become locked in battle over control of the interview. The scenario allows a modicum of breathing space for both parties. The candidate takes the lead, having the benefit of advanced preparation and creative control over the presentation, while the committee can devote a full 10-15 minutes to just intently listening.

The one caveat I might offer with respect to using a scenario in an interview situation is that the candidate must be told clearly and in advance that the scenario is *not* a fully developed bibliographic instruction presentation. It is an *outline* of a presentation, designed to highlight how one might approach a subject, a class, a specific instruction situation. The search committee must make its expectations crystal clear and not hesitate to call time if it appears that the candidate has exceeded the space allotted for the presentation.

EVALUATION AND TRAINING

Recruitment and hiring of new librarians is but the beginning in the personnel process. Once the newly hired librarian is in place, the real personnel issues begin to surface. New librarians, whether fresh out of library school or seasoned professionals new to the library, need and deserve careful orientation and training. In order for an instruction program to succeed it must be just that, a program, not merely a disjointed collection of activities, without philosophy or focus, that fall loosely under the rubric "bibliographic instruction." To ensure a quality program a great deal of attention must be paid to evaluation and training of all program participants, particularly new staff, and to the development of goals and objectives for the program.

The training/retraining and evaluation components of library instruction programs are, as in all things related to professional activities, sensitive issues. Many librarians involved in bibliographic instruction are "self-taught." By that I mean that they acquired their classroom skills through actually teaching, generally unsupervised. It becomes the responsibility of the reference department head (in cooperation with the instruction coordinator) to convince individual librarians of the necessity and advisability of improving and refining their classroom skills. Therein lies a multitude of potential personnel problems.

Reference departments frequently offer an interesting mix of individual styles and abilities, not to mention length of time in the profession or at the particular library. Many reference librarians predate the introduction of bibliographic instruction in their libraries. The mix of talent and interest, youth and experience, fiery enthusiasm and burnout, combined with the demands of an additional functional area, instruction, may wreak havoc in the library. When we add the possibility of evaluating classroom performance to that potent brew, real problems may arise.

The fact is that library instruction programs and instruction librarians need constant evaluation. Our students change, our collections expand (or occasionally contract), and technology is changing the face of the library. Evaluation of an instruction program extends far beyond needs assessment; it entails evaluation of individual librarians involved in the program, and that often requires each librarian-instructor to agree to participate in the effort to maintain or improve the quality of the service. Unfortunately there are no easy answers or pat solutions to the question of how to evaluate teaching. Teaching is a uniquely personal undertaking with few clearly delineated rights or wrongs. In our attempts to evaluate classroom performance we frequently confuse style with substance, thus reducing the whole enterprise to a subjective assessment. But we do ourselves, our colleagues, and our programs a greater disservice if we shy away from grappling with the thorny issue of evaluation. If the review of reference librarians actively involved in instruction ignores that aspect and concentrates solely on performance at the reference desk, how does the librarian-instructor know when she or he needs guidance, deserves special praise, or might well be directed to another type of activity.

One possible solution to the problem of improving librarians' teaching skills may be found in the development of a clear set of goals and objectives for the instruction service and their connection to a comprehensive training program for all instruction librarians.[4]

In-service training, while hardly a guarantee of quality or even standardization, provides individual librarians with the tools to improve or enhance their teaching ability. The more familiar we are with concepts and sources, the easier it becomes to share that information with others. In-service training affords the opportunity to both learn and teach, particularly if the role of instructor is shared among all reference librarians.

A comprehensive in-service training program can accomplish three major goals. The first and most obvious is that librarians are introduced to, or reacquainted with, new, unusual or difficult sources, strategies, or conceptual approaches to bibliographic instruction. Secondly, individual teaching styles are shared, and we learn both by doing and by watching others. The third goal or benefit is somewhat less obvious, yet potentially the most important of all. The sharing of skills and expertise with colleagues, or the collective working out of the most effective method for presenting material, may break down isolation and help to foster a sense of shared commitment to the educational mission of the library. It is during these sessions that the group might also address the issue of burnout and together come to some resolution of the problem, often by simply redistributing (or more equitably sharing) the instruction workload.

SHOULD ALL REFERENCE LIBRARIANS TEACH?

On a less collegial and optimistic note, I turn now to the single most pressing personnel issue in any instruction program: who should be teaching. All other issues pale when compared with the problem of determining how the library presents itself to the rest of the campus in that most revealing arena, the classroom. The problem must be addressed on several levels because what is "good" for the individual librarian may be detrimental to the instruction program (or to the library). On the other hand, our resources are often stretched to the limit and if we are to continue to provide bibliographic instruction, we may not have the luxury of encouraging some librarians to teach while actively attempting to divert others to less public-performance oriented activities.

The question of "to teach or not to teach" is a particularly complex one for academic reference librarians. Many of us have faculty status in our institutions; this may create an external pressure that we "behave" as much like teaching faculty as possible. For others, the perception that the librarian functions we perform are somehow less valid than those undertaken by other academics, puts us in a defensive posture vis à vis our colleagues on the faculty. The only response seems to be that we, too, teach.

In terms of the reference department, librarians are frequently responsible for bibliographic instruction because they are responsible for a certain portion of the reference collection or conduct liaison activities with specific academic departments. Occasionally instruction responsibilities fall to an individual librarian because she or he has a degree in the subject.

None of these seem particularly compelling reasons for all librarians to teach. In fact, given the far reaching negative impact that a poor performance may have on the library, just the opposite is true. Librarians with a commitment to quality teaching should represent the library in the classroom, others should not. But, how do you judge, where do you draw the line, how do you maintain quality in the face of escalating demands? The answer may lie in analyzing the causes of reference librarian burnout.

At the beginning of this paper I stated that poor allocation of personnel resources was as serious an issue as inadequate resources. The question of the responsibility for provision of quality library instruction is clearly a question of allocation of resources. Reference departments and library administrations need to set goals for instruction programs, keeping in mind the four areas touched upon in this paper: administration of the program, hiring of new personnel, training and evaluation of instruction librarians, and most importantly, the question of who should teach. Some reference librarians are uncomfortable with the expectation that they teach. Perhaps we are being too facile when we lump every personnel problem under the rubric "burnout." These individuals may have all the energy necessary to do most reference jobs, but neither the interest nor the skills to teach.

Bibliographic instruction *per se* is not a villain in the saga of burnout in our reference departments. But the tendency is to focus on it rather than taking the difficult steps of investigating what might truly be going awry. A careful analysis of what is actually happening in a reference department, determining strengths and weaknesses, both of programs and personnel, might help clarify the direction for the department and its myriad services. If, after this analysis, bibliographic instruction still appears to be causing more than its share of departmental woes, it may be time to reallocate personnel resources or alter the administrative structure of the program. The personnel issues brought to the fore by an active instruction program are sensitive, but not insurmountable. Careful assessment and the willingness to act to insure a quality instruction program may reveal creative solutions to stem the tide emergent burnout.

REFERENCES

1. William Miller, "What's wrong with reference: coping with success and failure at the reference desk," *American Libraries*, 15:5 (May 1984): 303-322.
2. Fromm, Roger W., "Tuesday morning live—personality and bibliographic instruction," *Directions for the decade: library instruction in the 1980's*, ed. by Carolyn Kirkendall, Proceedings of the Tenth Annual Conference on Library Orientation for Academic Libraries, Library Orientation Series no. 12. Ann Arbor: Pieran Press, 1981, p. 31.
3. Anne K. Beaubien, Sharon A. Hogan and Mary W. George, *Learning the library: concepts and methods for effective bibliographic instruction.* New York: Bowker, 1982, see particularly chapter 11, Administrative climate. This book fast became a standard in library instruction. Chapter 2, "Setting objectives" is also *highly* recommended.
4. Beverly Renford and Linnea Hendrickson, *Bibliographic Instruction: a handbook*, New York: Neal-Schuman, 1980, pp. 10-13.

Microcomputer Continuing Education Training Will Assist Reference Librarians

Thomas E. Alford

Improved reference service has several important tasks ahead of it . . . of utmost importance being for reference librarians to include microcomputer training in their continuing education endeavors. There is a desperate need for continuing education of reference librarians because better reference service depends on better-trained reference librarians.

Many libraries have formalized and elaborate training programs. In most cases, a training committee, having been established is given the responsibility for developing a series of continuing education workshops. The training workshops are usually supplemented by some written training materials organized and developed into reference manuals.

A number of libraries have training programs for new staff members which focus on policies, procedures and collection familiarization rather than an explanation of particular sources. The training sessions are conducted by the more experienced members of the reference staff. The length of training before the new employee begins to work with the public varies from less than a day to two weeks.

Typically, continuing education training programs for the experienced staff consist of periodic staff meetings at which new reference tools are shared. Also, a number of libraries have utilized vendors such as the Commerce Clearing House or Dun and Bradstreet to conduct workshops on the use of their reference tools. A sufficient number of libraries have used either in-library or purchased videotapes for reference training sessions. These types of reference train-

---

The author is Assistant City Librarian, Los Angeles Public Library, 630 West Fifth St., Los Angeles, CA 90071.

ing programs will continue to play an important role in providing good reference service.

Varied though they are, they all fall short of the mark for the future if they do not include microcomputer uses and training. There is a need to accept and develop ways to provide computer-based and computer-assisted reference to book and periodical holdings for the patron both from within the library and from the library directly to the public. Future reference service must recognize what is happening in microcomputer technology and develop methods for its integration within basic reference services. There is already an increase in the number of microcomputers in libraries.

In the November 9, 1984, *Publishers Weekly:*

> On average, over a third of American public, school, college and special libraries currently use microcomputers, and another third plan to purchase them in the course of the next year, according to a study recently conducted for the R. R. Bowker Company. The study, prepared by McGraw-Hill Research, was based on questionnaires sent this summer to 3500 libraries, and it recorded a response rate of 55%. It found that 26% of public libraries were currently using microcomputers, 51% of college and university libraries, 41.1% of high school libraries, 31.5% of elementary school libraries and 37.9% of special libraries serving technical and business patrons. The installed base of micros was respectively 11,477, 7079, 49,280, 92,243 and 26,736. The Apple was overwhelmingly the machine of choice, trailed by Radio Shack and IBM. As to future plans, 26.7% of public libraries currently without micros planned to buy them in the 1985-86 period, 54.9% of college/university libraries, 33% of high school libraries, 29.7% of elementary school libraries and 37.6% of special libraries. Word processing was the most common use for the machines (averaging 45.7%), with statistical uses (22%), database management (21.4%), inventory control (18.4%), graphics (16.8%) and spreadsheet (14.1%) as runners-up.[1]

REVOLUTION IN LIBRARIES

Across the nation, microcomputer technology is revolutionizing a number of routine practices in libraries. Daily, new library systems are being installed placing microcomputer terminals on desks, giving librarians instant access to more up-to-date information. While some librarians cheer this impact, and are hard at work keeping pace with the new technology, other librarians are not supportive, and are unwilling to face up to the new and sometimes difficult challenge of learning the different kinds of technical skills required for success in the changing library environment.

Today's society has changed dramatically from what it was several decades ago and most likely more changes are ahead. As these sweeping changes, both technological and social, continue into the 1990's, libraries as well as librarians must be more ready to respond to that change. Just maybe, change will bring fewer problems if we adopt the viewpoint that education for a career in library and information science only begins with a master's degree. An MSLS is only a beginning and not an ending. Because of the continuous change in the nature and environment of the profession, and the variety of the positions a person holds during a career, continuing education is a prerequisite. This is certainly true if reference librarians wish to be part of present and future microcomputer applications in libraries.

Reference librarians need to be a part of the library's present and future computer service programs. It would be interesting to know how many reference librarians are aware of microcomputer developments mentioned by Library Automation Consultant Joe Matthews. Perhaps a more challenging question would be, are they knowledgeable enough about these developments to plan for their introduction into the library?

The 29th Edition, 1984, Bowker Annual of Library and Book Trade Information, states:

> In his March 15 *Library Journal* article on the state of library automation, Joseph Matthews noted over 30 microcomputer-based systems on the market, forming a third, and fast-growing presence on the library automation scene. These range from inexpensive software to run on the library's Apple or TRS to sophisticated interfaces capable of tapping remote data bases and networks.
>
> The micros are literally sprouting up everywhere. There are an IBM PC doing periodicals work and an Apple handling service to the blind at the Tucson Public Library; an Osborne doing newspaper indexing at the Niagara Falls Public Library;

a TRS doing reference standing orders in Lorain, Ohio; and library micro user groups all over, with names like MUGLNC, PAMUG, and even SMUG.

Microcomputers are making conversion of library records inexpensive and fast in projects like Wisconsin's MITINET and REMARC's many conversion jobs. They are moving into action as superior terminals for OCLC, providing teaching support at Texas A&M, helping children with their studies at the Scottsdale Arizona, Public Library and in North York, Ontario, briefing new users on the library in Providence, Rhode Island, and offering inner city unemployed a new skill to learn in Baltimore. Apple programs can be borrowed by mail in Wenatchee, Washington, and entrepreneurs are offering coin-operated machines that cost the library little or nothing.[2]

ONLINE SERVICE

Online catalogs and online reference are a part of present-day library information resources. Print no longer comes on pages but in various formats such as microfiche and video screens. The use of microcomputers in the next decade may have equal importance with today's favorite reference tools. Indeed, by the end of this century, many more, not fewer, computers will be found in libraries, according to some predictions.

All around us in both the public and private sectors, officials are examining various methods using the microchip wizardry to spur economic growth and to have workers share the rewards of microchip technology with users. Now is also the time for reference librarians and other information specialists interested in improving access to reference sources to reassess the traditional reference assumptions related to reference services—not only focusing on source materials produced and distributed by the federal, state and local government information sources, but publications and reference works by profit organizations.

This review needs to address issues dealing with trends and strategies as they relate to public access to information when public access is viewed within the context of bibliographic control, collection development and resource-sharing, the role of new technology, reference and referral service and, finally, administration of collections and services. The review should be established to meet the following objectives:

1. To identify and discuss critically important issues related to increasing access to information.
2. To offer solutions and recommendations by which reference services can be made more effective.
3. To emphasize the importance and need for a research basis related to reference and information services.
4. To encourage a critical assessment of current practices and traditional assumptions related to reference services.

Such a review could lead to additional reference seminars and workshops which should provide insight into potential use for micros and data terminal equipment that the library already owns, as well as for future expansion. The workshop should be designed as an overview of basic concepts and issues relating to microcomputer systems. The objectives of this type of training should be to familiarize reference librarians with the many different types of microcomputer hardware and software systems.

Staff needs to meet in a training environment to learn about techniques to increase the effectiveness of reference collections and reference services. Training topics should include the impact of micros on collections and services, collection development techniques, evaluation of collections and reference services such as:

1. Provide an overview of methods for library assessment, the effectiveness of reference collections and reference services.
2. Suggest specific strategies by which reference collections and reference services can better resolve the information needs of patrons.
3. Demonstrate techniques by which collections and service goal objectives, performances measures and policies can be developed.
4. Provide an opportunity for staff to exchange views, ideas, information and strategies, developing effective reference collections and services.

The present-day use of data base searching using micros in the science field serves as an example, for data base searching is quickly becoming one of the primary reference tools available to reference librarians. This is especially the case for problems that are too current for monographic sources, such as in medicine, a field which depends especially upon the latest information. A microcomputer connected with a data base can put at your fingertips medical publications and do it fast, which is essential for those reference librarians who deal with patrons who want or need the results yesterday.

The National Library of Medicine MEDLAR System is such a data base vendor and is available to library members through METROMED and can be accessed by a micro. NLM's MEDLAR System is an overall program which controls a number of data bases that are unique in the medical sciences. Probably the best known is MEDLINE which is simply INDEX MEDICUS in an online format. MEDLINE is a bibliographic data base which gives the searcher access to some 3,000 world medical journals, from 1966 to the present. Other popular data bases in MEDLAR include Cancer Line, CLINPROT, HISTLINE, BIOETHICS, and EIRLINE. These are but a few of the data bases available under the MEDLAR System. Others include TOXLINE, Health Planning and Administration, ABLINE, SERLINE, and CATLINE, some 20 in all.

There is a need to be in touch with the latest trends, sources of information and contact people in this area of activity. Seminars, workshops and conferences offer an effective and concentrated way for reference staff to become current with what is happening in the micro field.

It is to be hoped that reference librarian training will help bridge the gap between existing services and current trends as the future of libraries and information agencies may be irrevocably linked to the successful building of that bridge. Continuing education training can assist librarians.

Reference librarians interested in microcomputer applications in libraries come from a wide variety of backgrounds, yet they have one common goal: to insure the quality of library microcomputer programs. Reference training programs can make a difference in the quality of the library's computer services. The support generated by knowledgeable staff members can provide the margin of excellence that can turn a good program into a great one. Reference librarians familiar with microcomputer procedures and resources are becoming increasingly more valuable library staff members as they offer advice and assistance in solving some of the microcomputer problems that arise in providing quality reference service.

As I look to the future, there is a need to do more—for we are in an evolutionary age and changes do come fast. How true when one looks at microcomputer use in libraries.

REFERENCES

1. PW At a Glance, "Microcomputer Use in Libraries," Publishers Weekly, November 9, 1984, Vol. 226, No. 19, p. 10.
2. Bowker Annual of Library and Book Trade Information (New York Bowker, 1984) p. 21.

Empirical Indications for Choosing Reference Librarianship as a Profession: A Biographical Approach

Martin H. Sable

Is it possible to identify potential reference librarians among high-school and college students, based upon the kinds of assignments they choose to undertake, and upon their hobbies? Given the opportunity, why do some students prefer to compile a bibliography or directory, when the majority of their peers opt for the essay approach? Furthermore, how many bibliographers have been "collectors", whether of matchbook covers, stamps and coins, dolls or barbed wire? May we postulate that the typical bibliographer is by nature a collector of something or other? The author is or has been a collector, a reference librarian, a bibliographer and a teacher of reference service, and he posits the following hypotheses: (1) that high-school and university students who, when offered a choice of type of assignment, irrespective of course, compile bibliographies or directories, as a minimum have the makings of reference librarians (and indeed, may enter our field); and, (2) given the "collecting" nature of bibliographic compilation, that most bibliographers either are or have been collectors, in their avocational pursuits. Of all human beings in the world, each of us has the most experience with himself (herself); I therefore shall base my arguments on my personal student and career life-histories. In addition, I intend to refer to myself in the third person, "he". A final request: since this essay is chronological, the facts and factors substantiating my two "educated guesses", as set forth in the two above-mentioned hypotheses, are intertwined.

Professor Sable is on the faculty of the School of Library & Information Science, University of Wisconsin-Milwaukee, Milwaukee, WI 53201.

© 1986 by The Haworth Press, Inc. All rights reserved.

PRIMARY-SCHOOL EXPERIENCE

At age 10, the student became fascinated with stamp-collecting as a hobby, bought a beginner's stamp-book at the then-current twenty-five cent price, along with a ten-cent magnifying glass, stamp hinges, and a 25-cent packet of H. E. Harris and Company assorted stamps, "international in scope". These actions were the typical ones: the real question worth pondering is why he was as fascinated with the still-standard reference work in philately, Scott's *Stamp Catalogue*,[1] literally spending days poring over its contents. While all stamp collectors refer to Scott's and must respect its authority, they typically do not spend as much time with it as with their own collections; the student-collector in question, however, did do so, and the question as to why, remains. Perhaps, if memory serves, the elements of political history (we know that political and historic achievements are reflected in stamps), combined with the element of "far-away places", all to be found in one book, alphabetically arranged by nation, provide a key.

JUNIOR-HIGH SCHOOL EXPERIENCE

The encounter with another reference book, at the age of fourteen, did not occur in junior-high school; perhaps the fact that it did *not* occur in a school setting reinforces the first hypothesis. During vacations, the student assisted his father, who was (in the pre- and post-TV era), a distributor of radio parts and equipment. One day he happened upon a book,[2] a section of which at that time, contained names and addresses of thousands of "ham" radio operators, with their call numbers, throughout the United States and in foreign countries. For many years following that first encounter, he would thumb through that section, simply as a pastime, reading the names and addresses of the amateur radio operators who were members of the American Radio Relay League. The student was not a "ham", and was not interested in becoming one: what, then, was the attraction for this technical handbook's *directory* section?

The author might play "devil's advocate", by suggesting that many people are interested in directories: his wife's colleague is a woman who maintains a collection of the *Yellow Pages* telephone directories of many cities. Nevertheless, how many people do you know who have such an interest? (Note: the colleague is not a Librarian, nor does her work partake of the nature of Library and Information Science).

HIGH-SCHOOL EXPERIENCE

As a 17-year-old high school senior, the student was to write a report for chemistry class. The instructor had suggested a wide range of topics, and indeed the student's peers selected topics ranging from chemical warfare to chemical engineering, as well as the contributions of individual chemists. Why, then, did he elect to compile a list of words and terms from chemistry, used in the Bible? Whatever the reason, the instructor approved his choice, and the student proceeded to contact the American Chemical Society and the American Bible Society, ultimately being referred to a chemistry professor at a midwest college,[3] who corresponded with him regarding the topic, since the latter had recently presented a paper entitled "Biblical Chemistry". Animated and encouraged by his correspondence, and guided by his high-school instructor, the student patiently culled words and terms from the standard concordances then extant.[4] He did not then realize that his chemistry report[5] would become the first in a series of reference tools he would compile as one aspect of his chosen life's work.

How many high-school students, one wonders, are accustomed to purchasing *World Almanac* annually, merely for the vicarious experience of reading the miscellaneous data therein? After all, during the student's high-school years, fifty cents[6] equalled almost two hours of earnings at the then-recently-established thirty cents per hour minimum wage. It appears that reading through the *World Almanac* entirely, in addition to reading the biographical entries of famous Americans[7] of the time in *Who's Who in America* must have satisfied some innate urge "to look it up", as well as to collect information.

At this point, it should be stated that the student had never had a course in "The Use of the Library", for the simple reason that no libraries existed in any of the public schools which he had attended. Thus, the urge to utilize reference books was not taught or fostered, but appears to have been an inherent interest.

UNIVERSITY EXPERIENCE

As an undergraduate major in Romance Languages (Spanish and French), the student, who also elected German for two years and taught himself Portuguese (from his knowledge of Spanish), acquired a collection of foreign-language dictionaries for each language. Just as immigrants desiring to learn English "read the dictionary", he engaged in vicarious reading of foreign-language dictionaries. There was, however, a precedent for this activity: he had during high-school, read through, with the identical motive, a one-volume encyclopedia.

For a senior theme, the student chose to write on the empire of Maximilian I, Emperor of Mexico, who ruled Mexico with the assistance of Napoleon III of France. While the topic was extremely engrossing, especially in view of the economic and political ramifications involving Mexican debts to Great Britain and Spain as well as to France (the supposed cause for the initial political intervention by all three nations), not to mention the over-riding significance of the Monroe Doctrine, and the succeeding pressure placed upon France to withdraw (after Great Britain and Spain had done so), the central element for us to consider is the following: *why did the student feel it necessary to supply a fifteen-page bibliography* at the end of the thesis?[8] One might respond that the work might appear more scholarly with such a lengthy bibliography (hence worthy of a higher grade), but would not a five- or ten-page bibliography suffice for that purpose? Why such a lengthy, time-consuming bibliography, if not for the sheer joy of compilation, in a multiplicity of languages?

With respect to foreign languages, the author had also studied many years of Latin and Hebrew, as well as the previously-mentioned languages. As a result he developed a hobby of collecting words which he believed to have traveled from one language to another, extending to languages such as Japanese (which he later studied). The hobby resulted in a lexicon of words (i.e., a *reference tool*), which also encompassed Arabic, Dutch, Italian, Indonesian, and Rumanian. Did the utilization of linguistic interest derive from stamp-collecting, to be ultimately portrayed in a listing (or lexicon) of words with common origins?

GRADUATE SCHOOL EXPERIENCE

As a graduate student in Latin American Studies, the student became interested not only in Latin American Studies programs worldwide, but in addition, in area studies programs covering the other regions of the world. Whenever time allowed, he would peruse the college-catalog collection at the Boston Public Library, which was voluminous, making notes regarding programs, university locations, languages taught and degrees offered. These notes were eventually revised and compiled into a pamphlet,[9] which was never published. The fact that the pamphlet went unpublished did not deter interest, for two years after receiving his Library Science degree, the student compiled a similar directory (also unpublished), this time restricted to the United States.[10] But let us not get ahead of ourselves.

DECISION TO ENTER LIBRARIANSHIP

As a result of these compilations and of the interest which provoked them, it became evident, especially in view of the time and effort consumed thereby, that what was involved surpassed a simple transfer of stamp-collecting to "fact-collecting". The realization that librarianship was indicated as *the* profession appropriate to such a hobby first came to his wife, who had been previously employed as an Assistant at the Boston Public Library. Her suggestion was also based upon the student's interest in all fields of knowledge (a vital qualification for reference librarians). Subsequent to receiving his professional library degree, it was only natural that he obtained a position as Bibliographer-Reference Librarian; during four years in that position, at a university library, he compiled some 15,000 titles in twenty fields of the pure and applied sciences. The resulting bibliography,[11] published by G. K. Hall and Company, was utilized as an acquisitions tool by librarians, and as a quasi-library catalog by scholars: for one full year, he was gathering materials for it from the various science-technology libraries of the Massachusetts Institute of Technology, in addition to utilizing a host of printed sources.

POSITIONS AND PUBLICATIONS

Many of his evenings and weekends were spent pursuing his hobby of identifying materials, located in the stacks of college and university libraries in the Greater Boston area, in the many disciplines and interdisciplinary areas, of the Humanities, Social Sciences and Science-Technology as these related to the study of Latin America. He began with the Widener Library of Harvard, and eventually covered all of the other major university collections as well as those at the Boston Public Library. After moving his family to the Los Angeles area in 1963, he continued his compilation utilizing materials from the collections at USC, the California State University at Los Angeles, the Los Angeles County Law Library, and from the many specialized libraries and the Graduate Research Library at UCLA. This compilation activity, conducted part-time, was a factor in his eventual employment in a bibliographic and research capacity by the UCLA Latin American Center, which eventually published his bibliography.[12] In that Center he developed, as one component of his responsibilities, a specialized reference service, which not only served students and faculty engaged in Latin American Studies, but also aided students and faculty at colleges and universities nationwide; eventually, reference questions began to arrive from abroad, and were promptly answered. His major task at the Center involved compilation of reference works on Latin America, especially those which filled gaps in the reference literature. In addition to the above-mentioned bibliography on which he had worked for seven years, both full- and part-time, the UCLA Latin American Center published three of his additional reference tools, a directory and two bibliographies.[13]

It was at the Center that doctoral candidates in Latin American history, approximately twenty in number, requested the former student and at that time Research Associate, to acquaint them with the reference tools requisite for undertaking dissertation research. As a direct result, he built, introduced and successfully taught either the first, or one of the first such interdisciplinary reference courses in the United States. Entitled "Latin American Research Resources" (he designated its course number as Latin American Studies #200), the course currently enjoys a large enrollment of graduate and undergraduate students, majoring in Latin American Studies. It acquaints students with the major general reference sources as these relate to the study of Latin America, as well as significant reference tools in the Social Sciences and Humanities as they concern the study of Latin America. In 1968 he left UCLA to become Associate Professor in the School of Library and Information Science of the University of Wisconsin-Milwaukee, where he has also taught the course, in addition to teaching it at a foreign university.[14]

A full professor since 1972, he specializes in teaching reference courses, and indeed has introduced four courses never previously taught (all of them advanced courses, the most recent one being "Information Sources and Services in Business, Industry and Finance", which he first taught in 1982). He has continued his compilation activity, and in addition to the University of Wisconsin-Milwaukee,[15] Scarecrow Press[16] and Blaine Ethridge-Books,[17] both publishers of Latin American Studies reference works, have issued some of his compilations. Several additional publishers, over the years, have issued others of his reference tools,[18] and he continues to pursue his compilation-avocation, presenting papers at conferences and reviewing reference books, in addition to submitting articles to library science journals. The articles run the gamut of teaching methodology in bibliographic instruction in Latin American Studies,[19] teaching techniques in reference,[20] methods of bibliographic compilation,[21] to the situation of the professional librarian.[22] Reference works and journal articles germane to the topics listed above have been cited, and the "student turned professor" (who, incidentally, considers himself to be a perennial student anxious to learn), has, due to his avid desire to divulge reference data, published additional reference works and articles on diverse topics. He advises his students that Library Science may be combined with any discipline or applied field, and that those committed to compilation should follow his lead provided they are so inclined, and become contributing bibliographers.

CONCLUSION: THE HYPOTHESES REVISITED

It has been said that "the unexamined life is not worth living".[23] This paper has covered a fifty-year time span in the life of a bibliographer-reference librarian-reference teacher. Given the interests as they were evinced, the hobby activities as they were expressed, and the eventual entry of the student into the field of reference service in all of its aspects, the inevitable question presents itself: may it have been possible to predict the individual's entry into the profession? Empirically and logically, it seems to be so. Might the example be utilized as a baseline study and as a model for future in-depth investigations? Or is the core interest (i.e., collecting data and an avid interest in reference tools) insufficiently widespread for application, with resulting lack of subjects[24] for study? Whatever the decision might be, the reality remains that reference librarianship, if only in terms of recruitment, is in dire need of such studies. Furthermore, the results of any such investigations would benefit hundreds of thousands of persons, perhaps millions worldwide, who might find their true profession is librarianship. It is, therefore, hoped that this autobiographical report might kindle a spark of enthusaism in a researcher who will accept the challenge of the dual hypotheses.

REFERENCES

1. Scott Publications, Inc. *Standard Postage Stamp Catalogue (the Encyclopedia of Philately)*. New York: Scott, 1867-   (annual).
2. *Radio Amateur's Handbook*. Edition 1-   , Newington, CT: American Radio Relay League, 1926-   (annual).
3. Postal card, dated December 12, 1941, and letter dated January 13, 1942, addressed to the author from Professor John T. Chappell, Professor of Chemistry, Marion College, Marion, Indiana.
4. Hazard, Marshall C. *A Complete Concordance to the American Standard Version of the Holy Bible*. New York: Nelson, 1922, 1234p., and Strong, James. *Exhaustive Concordance of the Bible*. London: Hodder; New York: Hunt, 1894, 1340 + 262 + 126 + 79pp.
5. Sable, Martin H. *Chemistry in the Bible*. Report for Chemistry class taught by Ralph E. Wellings, Dorchester High School for Boys, Dorchester, MA, 1941-42.
6. During the student's high-school years, fifty cents was the price of *World Almanac*.
7. Examples of notable Americans of the period, who were of interest, included Jack Benny (real name, Benny Kubelsky), Nelson Eddy, F. Scott Fitzgerald, Harold L. Ickes, Joseph P. Kennedy, Fiorello La Guardia, Clifford Odets, Elmer Rice, Eleanor Roosevelt, and Robert Sherwood, as well as Alexander Woolcott, among others.
18. Sable, Martin H. *The Maximilian Affair, With Special Reference to the Confederate Colony in Mexico, and the Test of Strength of the Monroe Doctrine in Mexico*. Boston: Submitted to Professor Andre Celieres, course in French Civilization, Boston University College of Liberal Arts, Winter 1945-46, unnumbered pages.
9. Sable, Martin H. *Worldwide Directory of Area Studies Programs*. Boston: 1954, 42p. (unpublished).
10. Sable, Martin H. *Foreign Studies and Public Administration Programs in Educational Institutions of the United States of America*. Boston: 1961, 24 unnumbered pages (unpublished).
11. *A Select Bibliography in Science and Engineering*. Boston: G. K. Hall & Company, 1964, 556p. (Note: this work was issued under the name of the employing library; the compilation is mine).
12. Sable, Martin H. *A Guide to Latin American Studies*. Los Angeles: UCLA Latin American Center, 1967, 2 volumes (864p.).
13. Sable, Martin H. *Master Directory for Latin America*. 1965, 438p.; *Periodicals for Latin American Development, Trade and Finance: An Annotated Bibliography*. 1965, 72p.; *Communism in Latin America, an International Bibliography: 1900-1945, 1960-1967*. 1968, 220p.
14. During the 1972-73 academic year, he was a Visiting Professor at the Hebrew University of Jerusalem, where he taught the course in Spanish, in the Dept. of Spanish and Latin American Studies, to masters' degree candidates, who had emigrated to Israel from many Latin American countries. He also taught reference in that University's Graduate Library School, an American-oriented library school which offers a master's degree in Library Science.
15. The Center for Latin America, University of Wisconsin-Milwaukee, has published his *Urbanization Research, With Special Reference to Latin America: An Inventory* (Center

Discussion Paper #20), June 6, 1969, 21p.; *Latin American Agriculture: A Bibliography.* 1970, 74p.; *The Guerrila Movement in Latin America, an International Bibliography.* 1977, 57p. *Materials on Latin America for Elementary and Secondary Schools.* 3d edition, 1982, 7p.

16. The Scarecrow Press, Inc., issued the following reference works, general as well as Latin American in orientation: *A Bio-Bibliography of the Kennedy Family.* 1969, 330p.; *Latin American Studies in the Non-Western World and Eastern Europe, A Bibliography.* . . . 1970, 701p.; *Latin American Urbanization: A Guide to the Literature, Organizations and Personnel.* 1971, 1,077p. In 1973 Scarecrow Press also published: *International and Area Studies Librarianship: Case Studies,* 166p.

17. Blaine Ethridge-Books, Detroit Michigan, a specialist-publisher of Latin American Studies reference works, issued *A Guide to Nonprint Materials for Latin American Studies.* 1979, 141p., and *The Latin American Studies Directory.* 1981, 124p.

18. See *Exobiology: A Research Guide.* Brighton, MI: Green Oak Press, 1978, 324p.; *Latin American Jewry: A Research Guide.* Cincinnati: Hebrew Union College Press; New York: KTAV Publishing House, 1978, 634p.; *The Protection of the Library and Archive: An International Bibliography.* New York: Haworth Press, Inc., 1984, 183p.

19. Journal articles on bibliographic instruction in Latin American Studies include "Bibliographic Instruction in Latin American Studies", *Latin American Research Review* (14: 1), 1979, pp. 150-153.

20. See "Teaching General Reference by the Case Method" (In Kaula Festschrift Volume, *March of Library Science.* Edited by V. Venkatappaiah. New Delhi: Vikas Publishing House, 1979, pp. 459- 462); "Academic Librarians and the Teaching of Bibliography", *Wisconsin Library Bulletin,* November-December 1974, pp. 305-306; "Teaching Reference by the Smorgasbord Method", *International Library Review* (16: 3), 1984, pp. 271-283; "Substantive Factors for a Theory of Reference Service", *International Library Review* (scheduled for Volume 17, 1985).

21. See "Methods of Bibliographic Compilation in Latin American Studies", *Herald of Library Science* (19: 1-2), January-April 1980, pp. 18-22.

22. For the topic of the professional librarian and attendant problems, see "Society's Debt to Librarianship: A Suggested Recompense", *International Library Review* 14, 1982, pp. 169-183; "A Prescription for Professional Prestige", *International Library Review* 15, 1983, pp. 5-8; "Protection of the Librarian", *International Library Review* 16, 1984, pp. 103-123.

23. Plato, *Apology.* Source: Bartlett, John. *Familiar Quotations; a Collection of Passages, Phrases, and Proverbs Traced to Their Sources in Ancient and Modern Literature.* 15th edition. Boston: Little, Brown, 1980, p. 83.

24. Although the methodology utilized in this report is perforce autobiographical, the *biographical* approach is emphasized (as set forth in the report's title), in terms of in-depth studies of each subject's collecting-type hobbies, interest in reference tools of any type, and actual bibliographic compilations completed, when the subject has been offered this option at any level of his/her school career.

Definitions Help

Lora Landers

BACKGROUND INFORMATION

The Hennepin County Library serves the County excluding the City of Minneapolis which operates its own independent library system. The Library provides services through three area libraries, 23 community libraries, a bookmobile, deposit collections at nursing homes and correctional facilities, and mail service to the homebound. An appointed seven-member Library Board responsible to the County Board of Commissioners acts as a Board of Directors for the system. A Library Director—appointed by the County Administrator from the recommendations submitted by the Library Board and ratified by the County Board—directs and administers the activities of the Library department. There are three major divisions: Administrative Services Division, Public Services Division, and Technical Services Division. Each division is directed and administered by a Division Director.

The Area Libraries have collections of significant greater depth than the Community Libraries. The Southdale Area Library with its 230,000 books and AV materials, 1,688 periodical titles and 80,000 government documents, is the central reference, advisory and collection center for the system. It also has a Media Lab for production of audio visual information. The Brookdale and Ridgedale Area Libraries each house 120,000 books and AV materials, 500 periodical titles and extensive pamphlet collections. With their in-depth reference collections, they provide information services to the North and West suburban communities and back-up services to the Community Libraries in those areas. Each Area Library also has a Media Desk with a playback capability for slides, film strips, 8mm and 16mm films, cassettes, records, video cassettes and TV.

The twenty-three community libraries provide information and

The author is Deputy Director, Hennepin County Library, 12601 Ridgedale Drive, Minnetonka, MN 55343.

© 1986 by The Haworth Press, Inc. All rights reserved.

recreational reading through a wide spectrum of library materials and programs. A Mobile Library on a bi-monthly schedule in areas of the County which do not have a community library provides adult and juvenile books, 8mm films, phonodiscs and advisory services. HCL also provides homebound service for persons unable to go to a permanent library, deposit collections in nursing homes and related institutions, and libraries in the Adult Corrections Facility, the Hennepin County Jail, the Home School, and the Juvenile Detention Centers.

The headquarters of HCL is called "ATS" (Administrative and Technical Services) and is located in the same building with one of the area libraries. The "ATS" complex includes the Director, Deputy Director, Materials Selection Section, Personnel Office, Public Information Office, Public Services Division administration section, Technical Services Division and Administrative Services Division (Accounting, Payroll, Material Acquisition, Delivery System, Buildings and Grounds).

The Library has a dictionary catalog with all formats interfiled; 4 editions a year are published, each one on fiche and one in book form. It and HCL's other bibliographic products have been written about so frequently that a full description is not necessary here but it is a major reference tool. There is an on-line circulation system which provides agency location and status and system-wide reserves for almost 100% of the cataloged circulating items in the collection. The automated circulation control system has become a major reference tool. Daily delivery from the Administrative and Technical Services building to every library agency complements these access opportunities.

The Library is a member of the Metropolitan Library Services Agency (MELSA) which is composed of the 7 County Public Libraries and the two City Public Libraries in the Twin Cities (Minneapolis, St. Paul) area. Through this cooperative arrangement, there is reciprocal borrowing and access to reference services.

There are 409 FTE positions filled by 550 people. The budget, pending a 1985 salary adjustment, is $15,033,522 which is $25.28 per capita. The materials budget is $2,213,786 or $3.72 per capita.

		1984 Statistics
Circulation:	Adult	3,876,056
	Juvenile	2,373,090
		6,249,146

Cataloged Materials Collection:

	Audio Visual	Print	Total
Titles	19,610	171,395	191,005
Volumes	103,462	1,128,239	1,231,701

Information Contacts: 815,365 (LIBGIS definition used.)

Service Area

The 1984 population estimate for suburban Hennepin County is 594,570; according to the 1980 census the median household income was $25,133 and the median years of school completed was 12.4. HCL serves 42 communities with 4/1/84 population estimates ranging from 83,710 to 350. The Library has a profile of each community which it updates every five years. Public transportation is geared to the major shopping centers. Residents are very mobile and there is an excellent network of highways and roads.

Library Users

There are approximately 260,000 card holders. The Library is currently undertaking a user survey but it is easy to state that most of them are above the state and national averages in terms of education and economic security and contribute to and benefit from the widely heralded Minnesota Quality of Life.

TIERED SERVICE

The Hennepin County Library over a period of years has developed a service pattern which is tiered. The buildings, collections and staff complements are designed to provide different levels of service ranging from the smallest Community Libraries to the Southdale Area Library which "houses the central collection." (This term is used to emphasize the fact that library is not a main library in the traditional pattern of city public libraries.) Descriptions of the circulating and reference collections of each type of library as well as other documents define the levels of service.

The Southdale Area Library is the only agency where the reference and advisory services are separated physically. The two-story building—the only one in the system—has what is called the Popular Library on the first floor consisting of adult fiction, audio visual materials (except 16mm films), popular periodicals, new adult non-fiction, children's materials and media desk and media lab. The second floor has the reference collection, the circulating non-fiction collection, the non-circulating periodical collection and a selected Federal document depository. The "central collection" has no subject specialization.

THE REFERENCE LIBRARIAN

The title "reference librarian" is applied to only one position in the library: a senior supervisory position in the Information Services Section of the Southdale Area Library. *The information which follows is about non-supervisory librarians in the public service agencies including children's librarians.* This includes two classifications, Associate Librarian and Librarian. Associate Librarian is the entry level professional classification which requires a bachelor's degree including or supplemented by 28 semester or 42 quarter credits in selected library science courses. Librarian is the second level professional classification. Associate Librarians can be promoted into that classification with two years of professional experience, six months of which must be at HCL when specific competencies have been demonstrated.

The Associate Librarians and Librarians in public service perform a wide variety of tasks including collection maintenance but it is the tasks associated with the public service function which fit them into a broad definition of "reference librarian."

— Provide advisory service
— Provide information service
— Interpret and explain library resources, policies and procedures
— Plan and conduct group programs
— Provide orientation to library materials and services
— Prepare bibliographies and pathfinders

to and for patrons of all ages using the appropriate materials and resources.

The KSA's (knowledge, skill and ability) for the Associate Librarian classification as written in the County's job specification are: (1) some knowledge of library policies, methods and procedures; some knowledge of materials in several broad subject fields; some knowledge of cataloging and classification; some knowledge of reference materials; and (2) working ability to establish and maintain effective working relationships with others; some ability to select appropriate materials for patrons of all ages; some ability to instruct and train non-professional library staff in methods and procedures; some ability to write reviews, prepare bibliographies and interpret library resources and services to the public; working skills in communicating effectively with the public.

The proficiencies to be promoted from Associate Librarian to Librarian as identified in the Library's promotional rating form:

1. Working ability to operate within the stated policies and procedures of the Hennepin County Library.
2. Good knowledge of the goals and purpose of the Hennepin County Library.
3. Working ability to effectively communicate orally.
4. Working ability to organize work. This ability includes the setting of priorities, meeting deadlines and responding to peak periods of demand which may be high patron volume or increased project activity.
5. Working ability to use reference, review sources and bibliographic tools.
6. Working ability to provide library services to meet community interests and needs.
7. Working ability to teach others to use library materials/resources.
8. Working ability to respond to patron questions using the sources and formats available to Hennepin County Library staff.
9. Working ability to conduct reference and "readers" advisory interviews.

CONCLUSION

Based on thirty-five years of experience in four outstanding public libraries, this writer firmly believes that position specifications, service level definitions, job descriptions with functions and tasks, and performance objectives set in the framework of a library's goals are essential but they must be combined with:

— "read, read, read," described by Margaret Steig in her article in the December 15, 1980 *Library Journal*, "Continuing Education and the Reference Librarian in the Academic and Research Library" and "watch, listen and enjoy" which Carol Royce added in her letter about the article (LJ 2/15/81).
— an HCL information services policy: "Professional judgment and discretion take precedence over stated policies and procedures in order to best serve the Library's users."
— commitment to public service
— respect for each person
— being intrigued by the person's question or request when it is unique and by realizing that the repetitious question or request is unique to the person.

Selecting a Reference Librarian: Signs to Look For in Selection

Mabel Shaw
Susan S. Whittle

> WANTED: a reference librarian—
> swifter than Superman;
> cleverer than Doctor Who;
> undaunted by Sphinx-like riddles;
> wise as Solomon. Hopefully can even
> spin a little gold from
> straw in the evening.

Far fetched! Perhaps not since the virtues demanded of reference librarians often boggle the mind. How many other professions require "the pursuit of encyclopedic knowledge and the practice of a systematic research methodology, but also the skills of a diplomat, the counseling ability of a psychologist, and the physical and emotional stamina of an Olympic athlete."[1] Wyer[2] and Hutchins[3] both present extensive and awesome lists of characteristics of reference librarians. Wyer's list of 27 desirable traits begins with intelligence, accuracy, and judgement, and ends with patience, forcefulness and neatness. He summarizes his list by saying that "the ideal reference librarian must love Books, Folks, Order."[4] Hutchins considers a good imagination as important as a good memory with generous dollops of thoroughness, orderliness, persistency and observation tossed in. Both concede that the lists are comprehensive and that all traits are seldom found in one person.

Fortunately (since paragons can be difficult folks), the person eventually hired will be an ordinary person with virtues and shortcomings like all the rest of us. If this person is to be an effective reference librarian, however, he must be made up of that unique

---

Ms. Shaw is Reference Librarian, Tallahassee Community College, Tallahassee, FL 32301. Her co-author is Public Library Consultant, State Library of Florida, Tallahassee, FL 32301.

combination of personality and behavior traits that characterize reference people. So in addition to meeting the necessary requirements for a professional position, this new staff member should exhibit some special qualities.

RESPONSIBILITY IS BASIC

A sense of responsibility for reference work and an excitement in and commitment to the information process is basic. A good reference librarian enjoys the work and the variety of people, questions, and experiences it offers. He or she loves handling information—acquiring, storing, finding, and relating it to an individual's needs. A reference librarian likes and intuitively understands people and their foibles, and gains satisfaction from serving people and interpreting the library and its holdings to them. He or she is constantly attuned to the fact that the way in which a person's question is answered is almost as important as the answer itself. The reference librarian must be tactful, patient and responsive, and able to keep cool even when throngs of library users encircle the desk. Adept at communication and interpersonal relations the reference librarian must always be ready to meet the public with a sense of humor and a look of approachability.

A broad academic background and catholic interests go a long way toward helping the reference librarian meet the day's allotment of questions. Through a good general education and expertise in the use of the tools of research, the librarian is able to cross over many disciplines to locate citations and documents on a variety of subjects. In addition, he or she possesses a sound knowledge of the basics of standard reference sources plus a working knowledge of reference procedures and problems. It is necessary to be alert to social changes and new technology currently affecting reference sources and services and seek opportunities to learn the latest trends in reference work and librarianship. He or she functions effectively at the card catalog having developed an in-depth understanding of cataloging and classification schemes, understands the importance of monitoring and developing collections as well as learning their contents, and is an excellent bibliographer with an increasing interest in computer-based bibliographic databases. Comfortable serving as an intermediary and teacher through an expanding familiarity with literatures and their structures, he or she is, in Mearns' words, in the process of becoming the "master of materials."[5]

Besides having a broad academic background, the potential reference librarian is intellectually curious and has a zest for learning and constantly probes beyond the mere statement of words to the deeper meaning of the author who wrote them. In touch with the world, and seeking breadth of vision and knowledge in many subject areas, he or she is blessed with a good memory and an ability to connect seemingly unrelated pieces of information. No mere dispenser of unrelated facts, he looks beyond the obvious in each question and pursues the acquisition of new insight and has an abundant supply of persistence coupled with detective skills and a love for the hunt. Last, he perceives that, in a world of overwhelming information and subject knowledge, teamwork in reference services is an indispensible ingredient for success. A sense of professional courtesy stifles any temptation to blind others with his own brilliance. In fact, he or she keenly believes that interpersonal relationships with other staff members are as important as those between librarian and users.

There is a mystique about being a reference librarian, the link between the resources of the library and those who come seeking information. The ability to find information is a precious skill—the hallmark of excellence.

To the library user, the reference librarian's ability to "comprehend the relation between a given question and a given patron and to deal successfully with that relationship is indeed an art."[6]

DESIRABLE TRAITS

Interviews with 40 library users ranging in age from 18- 45 clearly showed the following traits to be desirable in a reference librarian.*

1. Ability to obtain the information needed quickly (top priority in all respondents)
2. Openness and willingness to help
3. Courteousness and sensitivity
4. Knowledge in subject areas
5. Imagination and intuition to lead users into other related areas

---

*Interviews were conducted with fifteen (15) people from each of two locations and ten (10) people from one location of Florida. The question asked was, "What traits would you like exhibited to you when you ask a reference librarian a question?" Each user had used the services of a library for reference purposes at least twice.

6. Persistence to find information if not readily available and make necessary follow-up to user
7. Sincerity and dedication
8. Tactfulness, diplomacy, and non-condescending attitude
9. Integrity

Those persons selected to work at the reference desk will determine the success or failure of a library's service to people. They, therefore, should possess in abundance those personal qualities and professional attitudes exhibited in the best of reference librarians.

REFERENCES

1. Hinckley, Ann. "The Reference Librarian." *College & Research Libraries News*, 41:62-64, March, 1980
2. Wyer, James. *Reference Work*. (Chicago, American Library Association, 1930): pp. 234-239
3. Hutchins, Margaret. *Introduction to Reference Work*. (Chicago, American Library Association, 1944): pp. 32-35, 160-162
4. Wyer, James. *Reference Work*. p.238
5. Mearns, David. "Master of Materials: Random Reflections on Reference Librarianship." in Rowland, Arthur. *Reference Services*. Hamden, Conn., Shoe String, 1964. p.181
6. Reed, Sarah. "The Reference Librarian." *Library Journal*, 81:21-23, January 1, 1956

ADDITIONAL SOURCES

Cox, Carl. "Return to the Basic Guides." *Tennessee Librarian*, 18:127-131, Summer, 1966
Halleman, W. Ray. "The Reference Librarian." *Special Libraries*, 52:314, July, 1961
Isaacson, David. "The Reference Librarian as General Fact-totum." *Wilson Library Bulletin*, 54:494-500, April, 1980
Katz, Bill and Fraley, Ruth. *Reference Services Administration & Management*. New York, Haworth Press, 1982. (THE REFERENCE LIBRARIAN, Number 3, Spring, 1982)
Reed, Janet. "The Reference Mystique, Part 2: What I Didn't Learn in Lib. Sci. 101." *Cornell University Libraries Bulletin*, 183:6-7, May, 1973
"The Reference Librarian." *North Carolina Libraries*, 22:89-90, Spring, 1964
Rothstein, Samuel. "Reference Service: The New Dimension in Librarianship." *College and Research Libraries*, 22:11-18, January, 1961
Schlachter, Gail. *Service Imperative for Libraries*. Littleton, Col., Libraries Unlimited, 1982, pp.157-68
Spicer, Carolyn. "The Reference Mystique." *Cornell University Libraries Bulletin*, 183:4-5, May, 1973
Turner, Stephen. "Relevant Reference Training." *Pacific Northwest Library Association Quarterly*, 40:15-17, April, 1976

For Product Safety Concerns and Information please contact our EU
representative GPSR@taylorandfrancis.com
Taylor & Francis Verlag GmbH, Kaufingerstraße 24, 80331 München, Germany

www.ingramcontent.com/pod-product-compliance
Lightning Source LLC
Chambersburg PA
CBHW052112300426
44116CB00010B/1634